# LINES OF MADNESS

# Lines of Madness

**KADEN POPE**

Kaden Pope

# CONTENTS

## HOPE & DESPAIR



## CALM & CHAOS

## REALITY & INSANITY

## COURAGE & DEFEAT



## INNOCENCE & PAIN

## AWARENESS & NUMBNESS

## PRIDE & SHAME

**For my Mom and Dad**

*Who never gave up on me,*
*even when I gave up on myself.*

# TRIGGER WARNINGS

Mental Health Hospitalizations, Suicide, Self Harm, Blood, Psychosis, Cutting, Isolation, Bullying, Grief (Loss of Parent), Depression.

# CONNECTION & OTHERNESS

# Sounds of a Dragonfly

Gazing longingly through the crowd.
Friends laughing,
children screaming.
Sounds vibrating
through me,
like a dragonfly.

Heart pulsating in my chest…
does anyone know that I exist?
Could I become part of this?

They dance instinctively,
flowing gracefully,
over…
under…
beside…
and through.

I wish I could be like them…
Connected to the world.

Goosebumps form,
filling my arms and legs…
imagining the joy of being free.
Dancing to the sounds of a dragonfly.

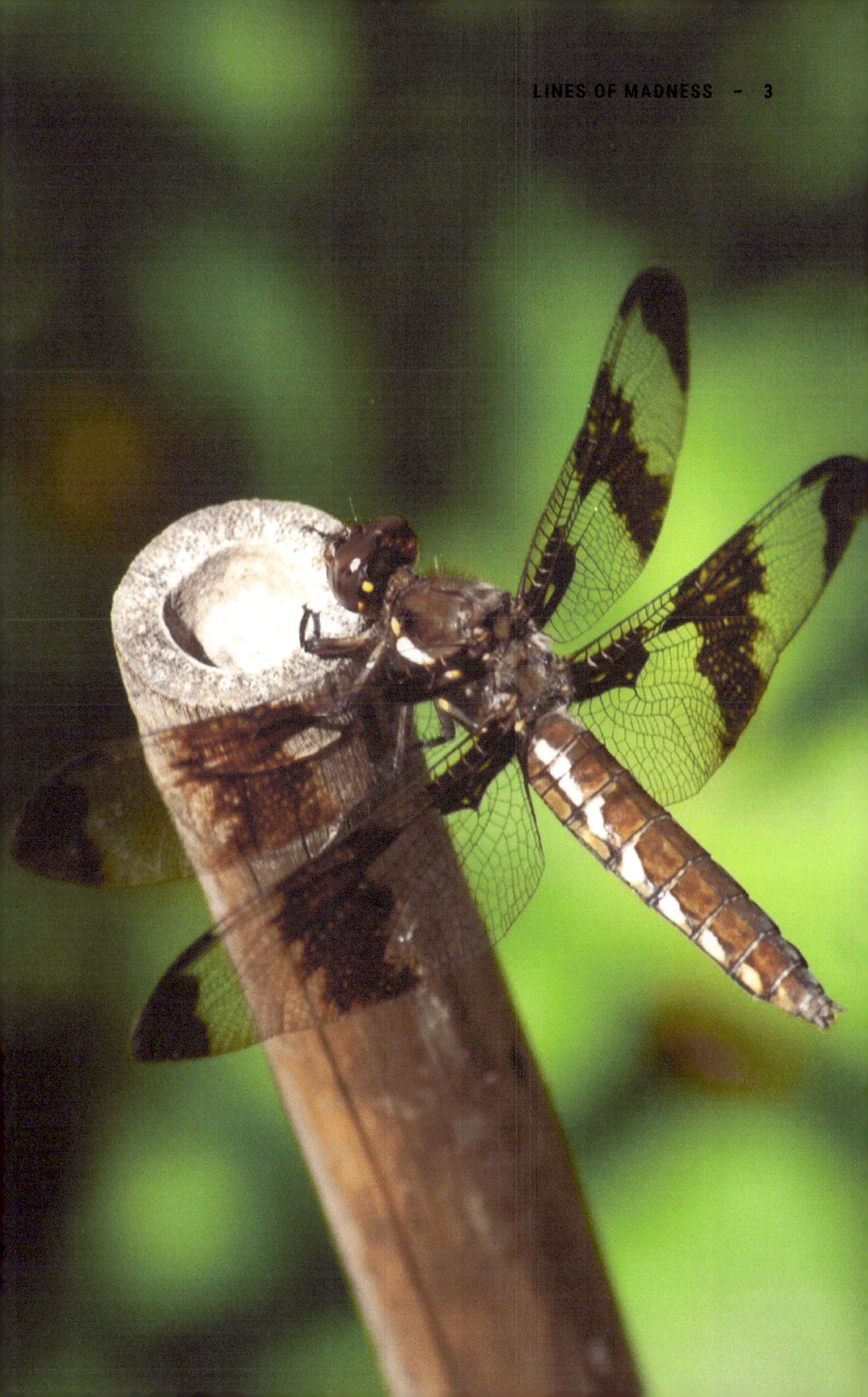

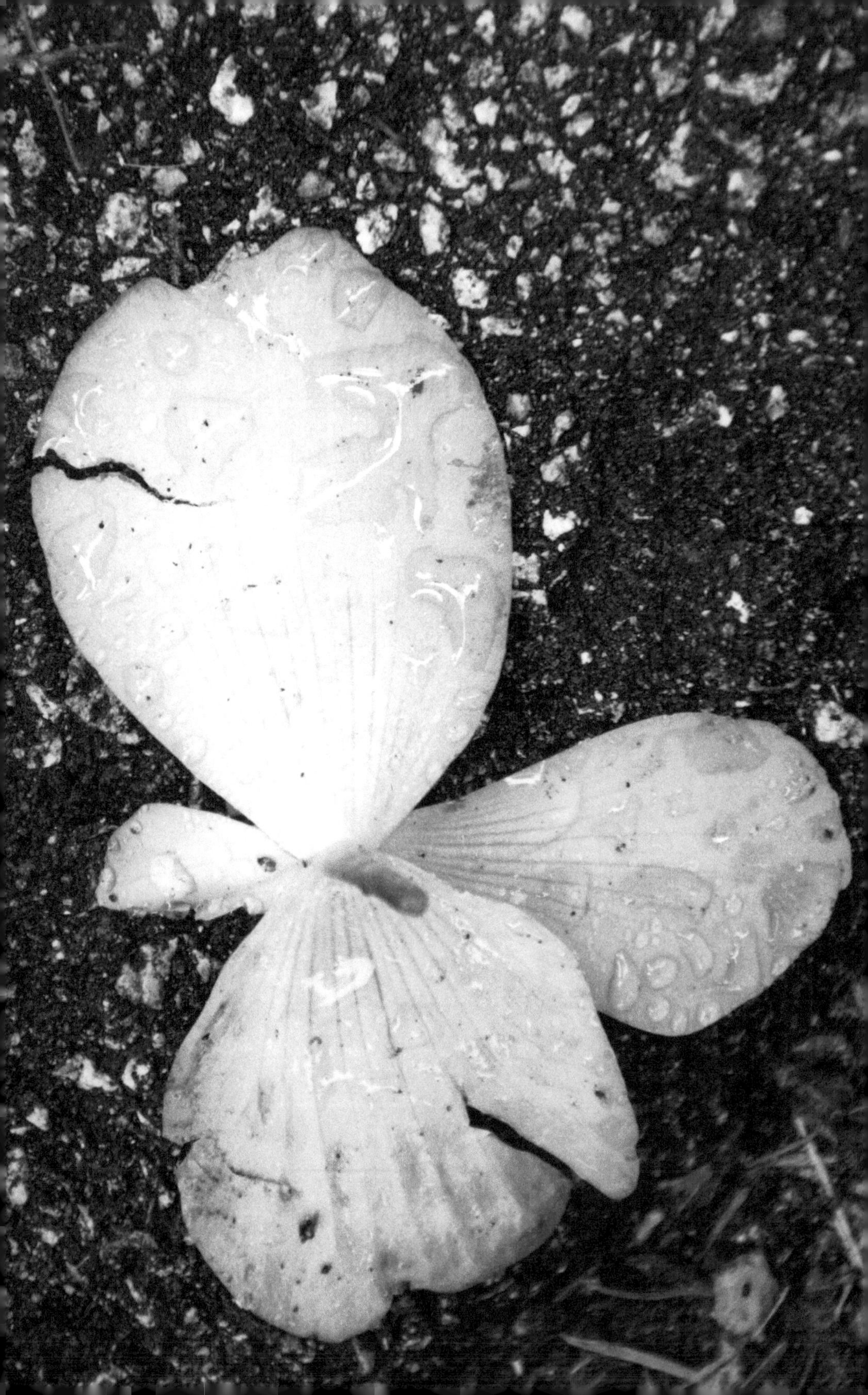

# Bullying

**B**eating up my heart inside,
**U**nknown to you, I want to die.
**L**ook away, the others say.
**Le**tting you win, I'm bruised today.
**Y**ou dish out hate.
**I**'m carrying a heavy weight.
**N**o! Stop mocking me!
**G**o away, I'm loving me as me!

# Stand Strong

Chin high,
shoulders back.
Taking up space
in my empty room.

I must show the world
that I am proud
to be myself.

*I hope deep inside that I look the part…*

Hours rehearsing
behind closed doors.
Desperately hoping
they don't see my fraud.

The door opens.
Slipping into the crowds,
I'm standing strong.

*No one knows what I hide…*

She looks my way.
Confidently I stand.
Looking her in the eyes,
I give a strong handshake.

She tells me her name.
Holding her hand firmly,
my knees feel weak —
she's talking to me.

*I can't do this anymore…*

I feel sick, body weak.
I run to the bathroom,
hiding my tears.

I slam the door…
desperately hoping
my sobs aren't heard.

Strength and confidence
fragmented like shattered glass.

*I can't be something that I'm not.*

# You Picked Me Up

One by one, I took my first steps.
Feet firmly planted on the ground below.
Soon I fell hard, scraping my knee.
Crying for help, I felt all alone…
*You picked me up.*

My first day of school finally came.
So proud of the time I spent out in the world.
When school became too hard to bear,
feeling like I wasn't good enough…
*You picked me up.*

Teenage years came all too fast.
I met great friends and loved them with all I had.
When friendships faded in painful ways.
Lost, inside and out, not knowing who I was…
*You picked me up.*

I went off to university, standing strong.
Life's problems piled high on my head.
Exhaustion filled my days.
I cried out confused, lost beneath the stress…
*You picked me up.*

It was time for me to take steps from far away.
School done; I was on my own.
I thought my first 'real' job would be the one.
Lost and confused, one week in, I quit…
*You picked me up.*

The world is a scary place, but do not fret,
be proud of who you've taught me to be.
When scared or lost I can call out,
knowing that my feelings aren't too big for you…
*You'll always be there to pick me up.*

*Thank you, Mom and Dad, for being there to pick me up.*

# Look me in the Eyes

Socks still wet from days before.
Shivering in the crisp winter air,
she hugs her knees.

Body aching, longing to be who she once was,
warm…
dry…
on par with humanity.

Sounds of footsteps come near.
She looks into his hazel eyes.
She longs for him to be the one.
The one, who returns her smile.

His eyes quickly dart away.
Her heart twinges – he is like the rest.

She drops her chin,
hiding her face.
Swiftly wiping away the tears
flowing down her cheeks.

Crumpling like a crisp autumn leaf...
her lips quiver, "Please, could someone just
look me in the eyes and smile."

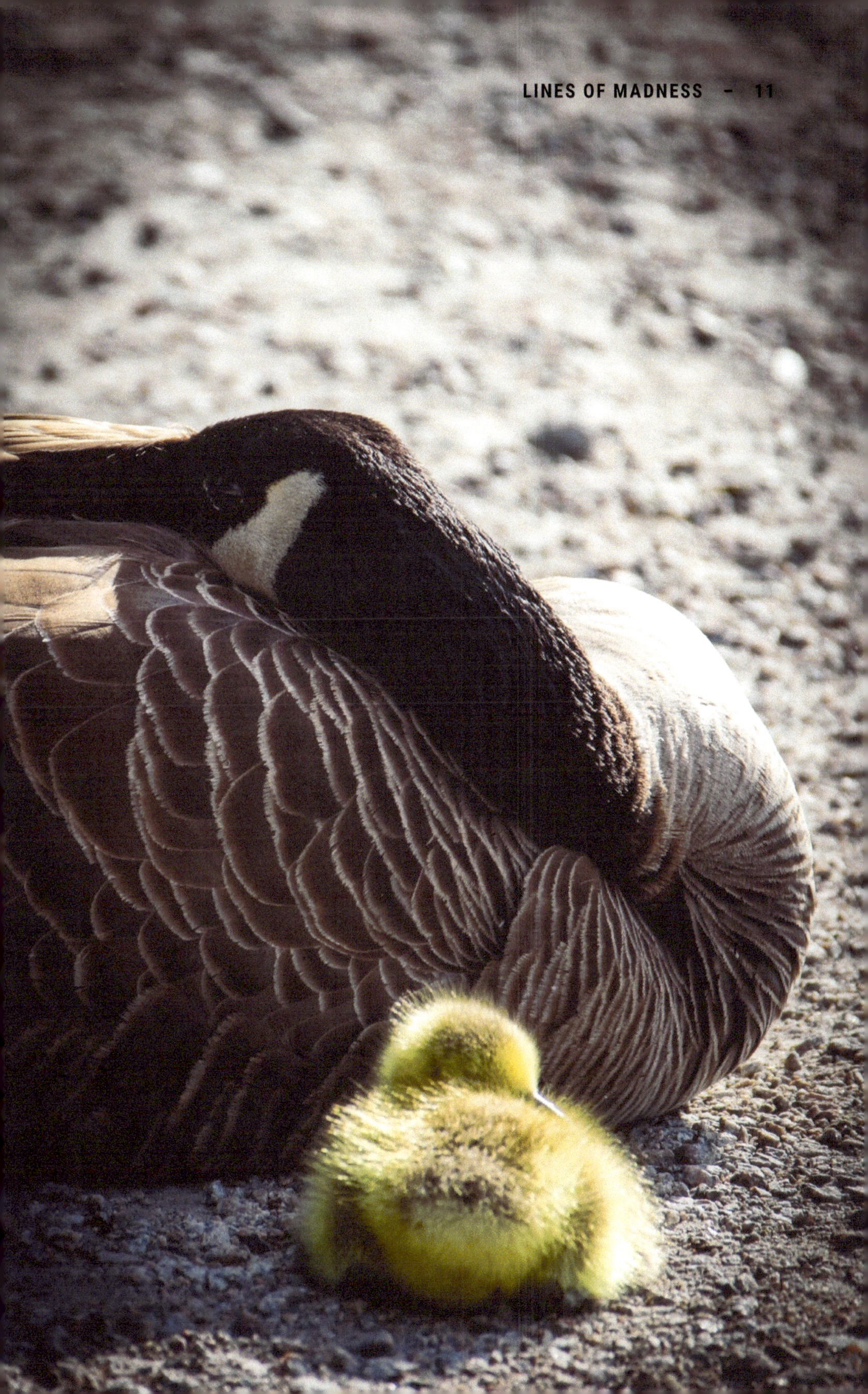

# Deserving

Shaking…
stuttering…
pleading to be left alone.

Standing…
apart…
emptiness fills the void.

Deserving…
loneliness…
living inside of me.

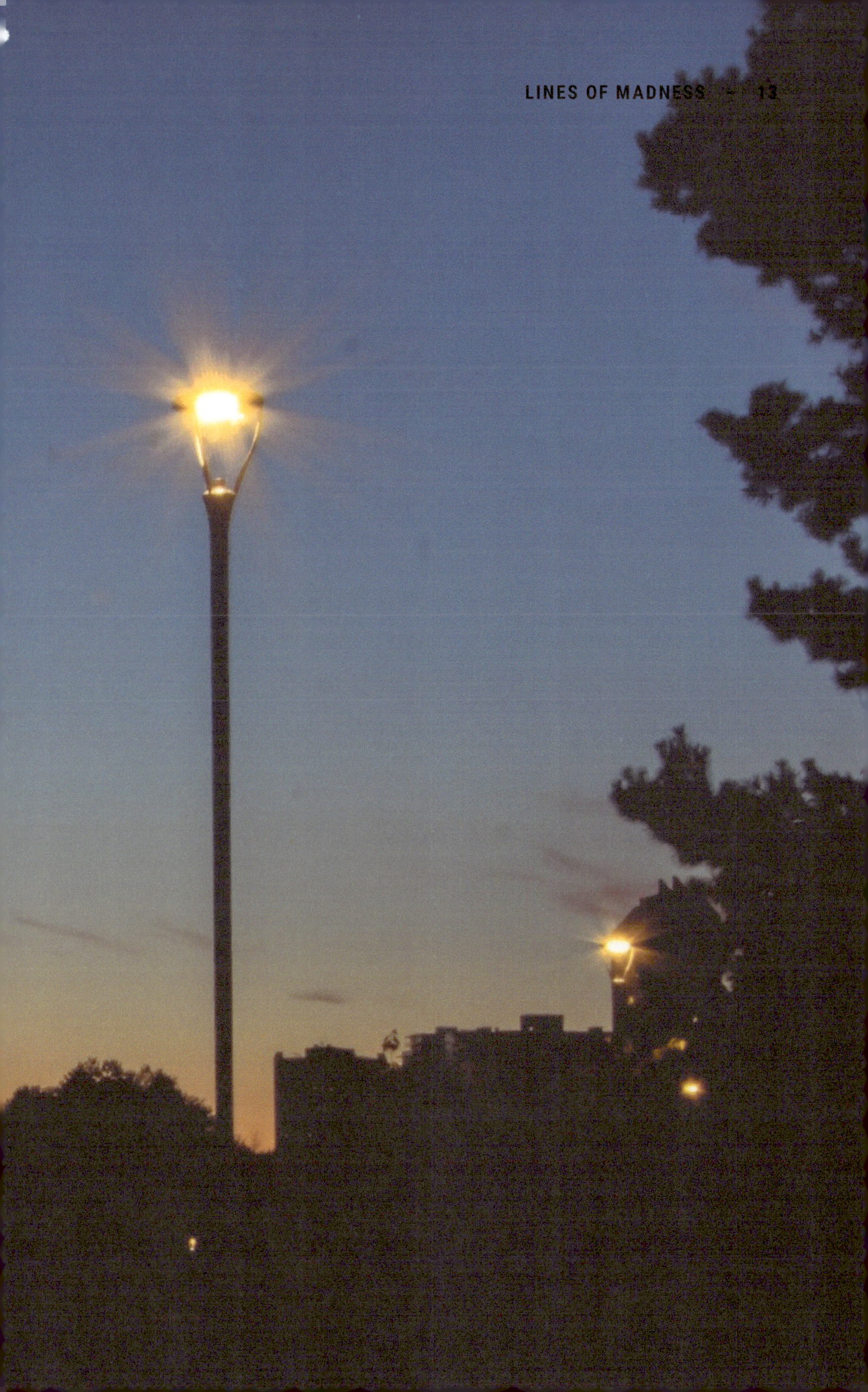

# Our Voice

These lines give light to a journey
of shame and fear,
of someone living with
evil in their bones.

A life once hidden
will come to life.
As I write my truth,
my voice explodes…
a new person grows to
push away my shame.

Proving doctors wrong.
I am determined become more
than the limits they put on me.

Through these lines,
I hope others listen
to the story aching in their bones.
Knowing they, too, are more
than the limits
of their diagnoses.

# Mailbox

Gawking at the line of metal doors,
your heart grasping for connection…
hoping to find something inside.
A letter, a cheque, or even a bill.

Anything would make your day.
This metal box is your connection
to the outside world…
A reminder that you are not alone.

Turning your key, you peek inside.
Releasing a heavy sigh,
you slam the door so no one sees
your empty box.

You are alone.

# Home for the Holidays

Home for the holidays,
one week till Christmas eve.
This will be her last season
to decorate the tree,
to make memories with us.

Nowhere inside did we know
that her body wouldn't
make it through the night.
She would be gone too soon
to decorate the tree with lights.

That night,
she died with us by her side.
Kissing her one last time,
I waved goodbye.
Knowing that her last Christmas,
had already passed.

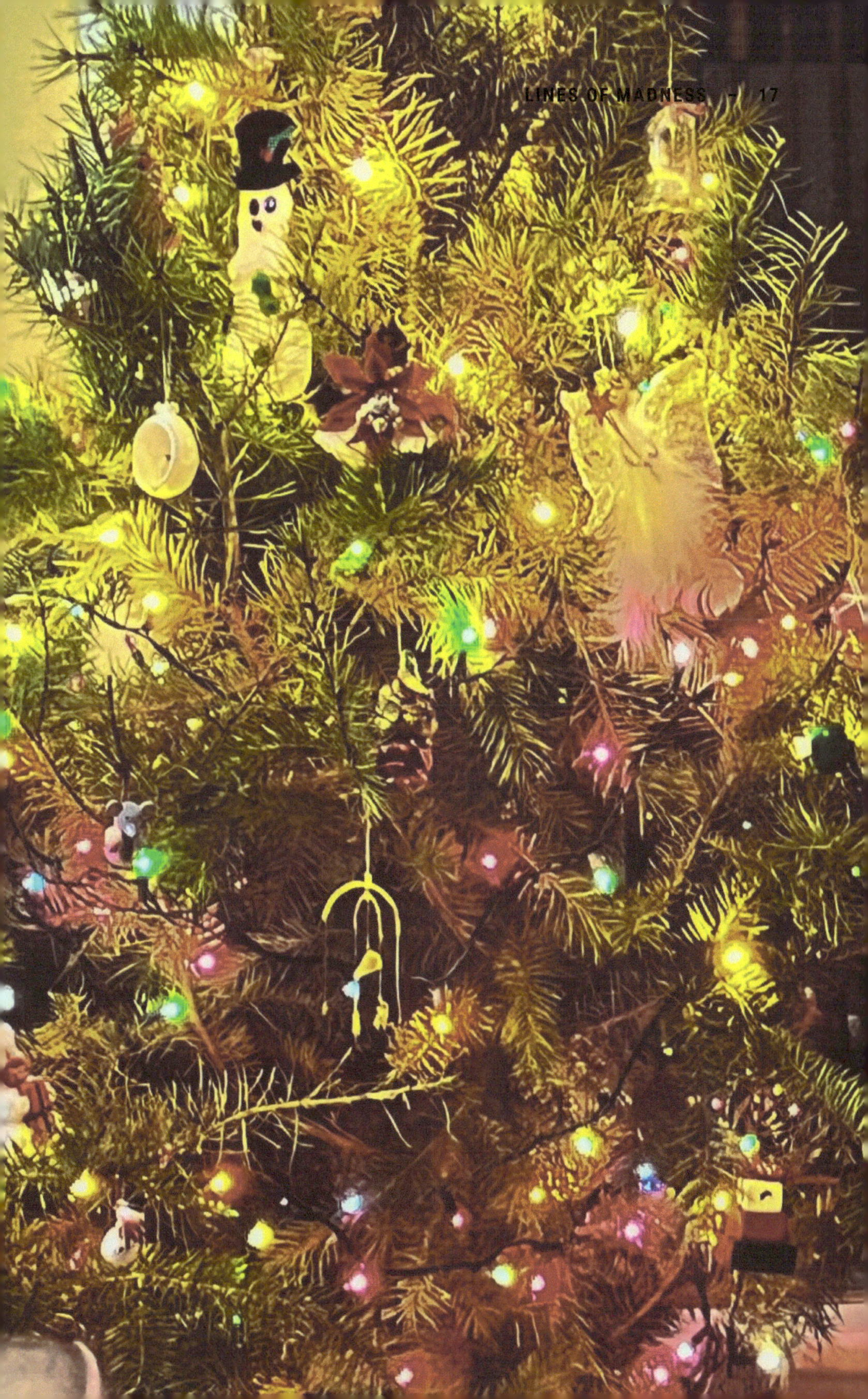

# Vulnerability

Revealing the wounds in my heart,
I tell my story without skin,
sharing a life of difference
and vulnerability.

Terrified, I whisper…
"I am not psychosis,
I am not depression,
I am not self harm."

I pause…
My identity is not
mental illness,
or the labels given to me.

Hopeful, I whisper…
"I am creative,
I am vulnerable,
I am strong."

Let this echo through your veins.

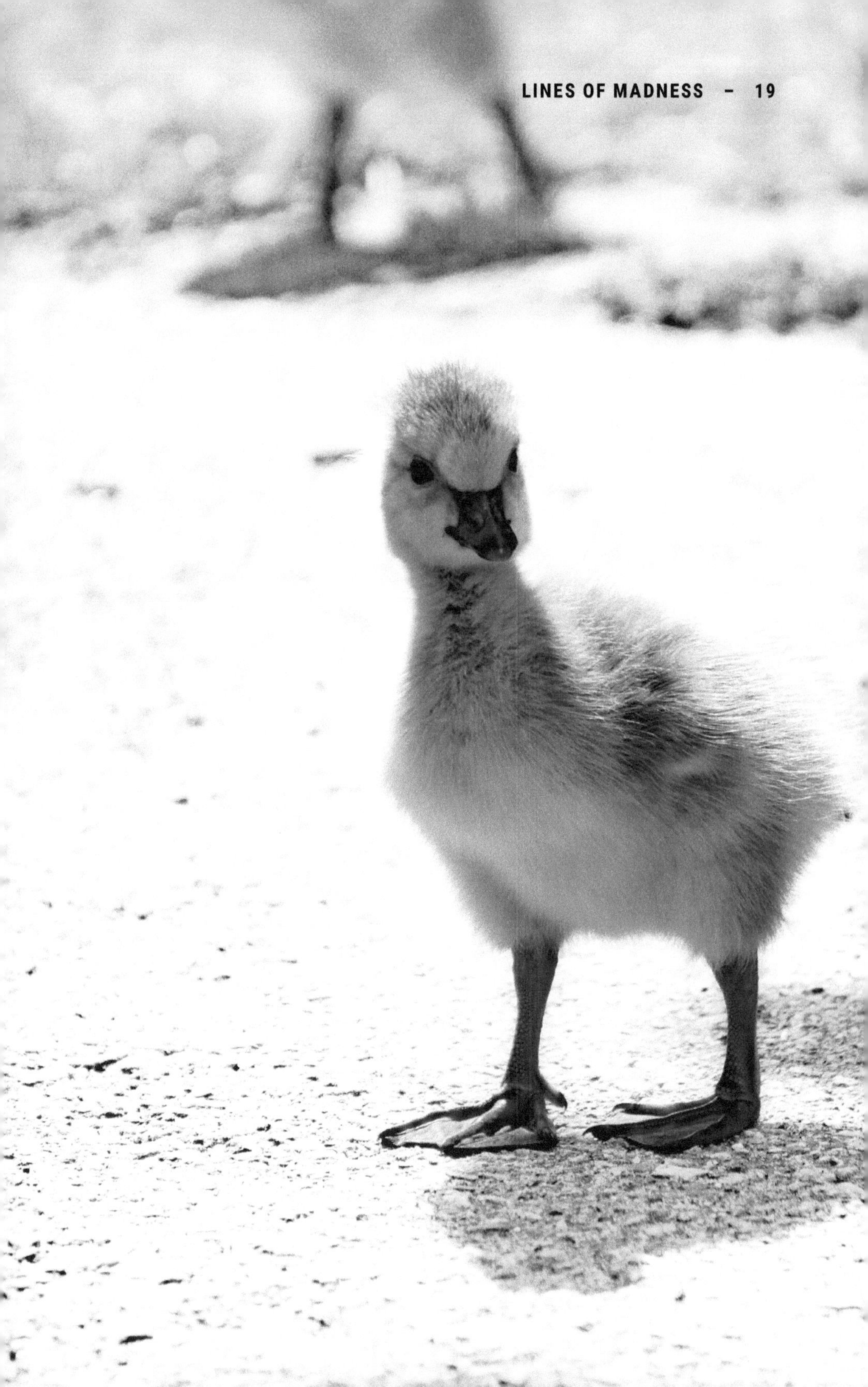

# HOPE & DESPAIR

# Insanity

The world I know transforms,
exchanged with echoes of reality.

Trying hard to look away,
I am entranced by what I see.

Blood creeps gently down the walls,
as fragmented paths emerge.

Crimson puddles flood the floor,
I watch the walls as they fade away.

As time becomes null,
I slip further into insanity.

Babies lie motionless on the floor,
drowning in their blood.

With no escape, my eyes are fixated,
lost in the world surrounding me.

# Death

Emotions gone.
Fighting back tears
that will not come.

On my knees...
my life explodes
inside of me.

Body searing...
I need it to end.

Cutting deep...
taming the pain,
sizzling inside of me.

Blood flows.
Hands numb.
This is my time.

Arms open.
Relief exhales
one last time.

This is it; I am done.

# ECT (Shock Treatment)

I sleep softly through the night,
as the morning breaks, I wait tight.
Away I'm wheeled to a secret floor.
Scared, am I? — No, not anymore.

They poke for veins they cannot find,
even asking their friends to find a line.
Five needles till they've found the one,
I'm ready — let's get this done.

Patiently waiting, I hope it won't be long,
for those before me to move along.
Doctors appear above my bed,
one marks lines atop my head.

"Ready?" He asks of his peers.
Nodding their heads — the world disappears.
My body weighs more than a ton,
I remember no more — the zaps now done.

They ask me who I am.
Lost, confused — I don't give a damn.
Soon, I know the day, month, and year.
Awake and tired, I know I am here.

Sitting up, the world around me clear.
My toast and jam quickly appear.
Patiently wait for the porter to show,
time creeps by while I wait to go.

Back on the ward — I head to bed,
hours later I awake with a little pain in my head.
Now ECT is not for all,
it may not change your life at all.

But it took away my blank and empty gaze,
helping me navigate a world that was once a maze.

# Heaven's Gain

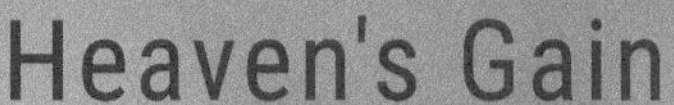

Understanding, drowning in a void.
Hopes, standing as an endless wall.
Dreams, now filled with your death.

This is not part of God's Plan.
He understands my need for you
is stronger than heaven's gates.

There is no reason to justify
why you were stolen away
A hope for a future,
now gone.

I had dreams
to make you proud,
to show you who I've become.
But mom,
I lost you before your time.

Your death was not
Heaven's Gain.

Pacing around my room,
I search for a life
that can never be found...

# Lost at Sea

Alone, I float in makeshift sail...
endless ocean encircling me.
For months, I've been gone,
longing for everything to end.

Knowing that those I love
no longer think of me.
Barely sleeping through the night.
Early morning, I see...
a glimpse of land ahead of me.

Could freedom be this near?
Floating closer, inch by inch.
Grinning ear to ear, I squirm.
Shadows moving up ahead.

Humans coming out to me.
Excitement builds and builds.

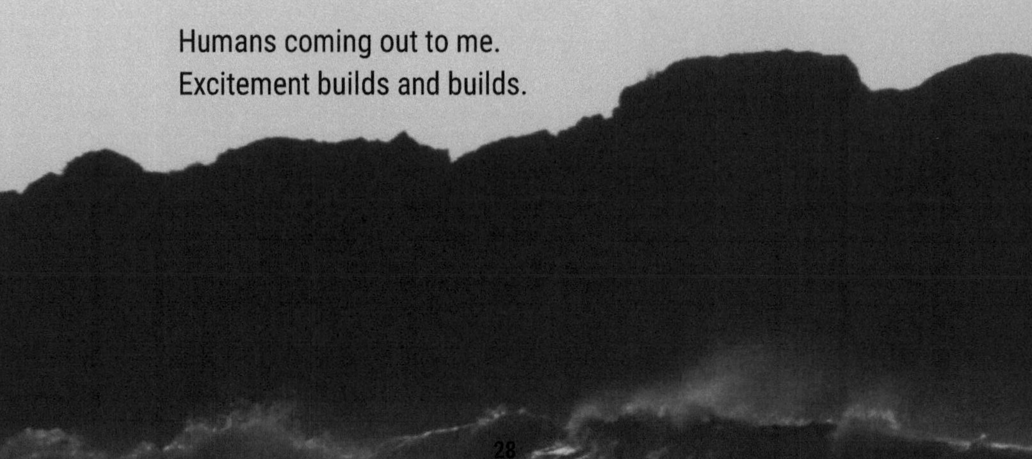

I need a place where others care.
A space to hold
my pain,
my loss,
my emptiness.

The closer I come,
the shadows grow.
I'm filled with relief so big
my knees let go.
They come swimming out,
supporting me onto land.

They care, they're calm
This place is safe,
for me.

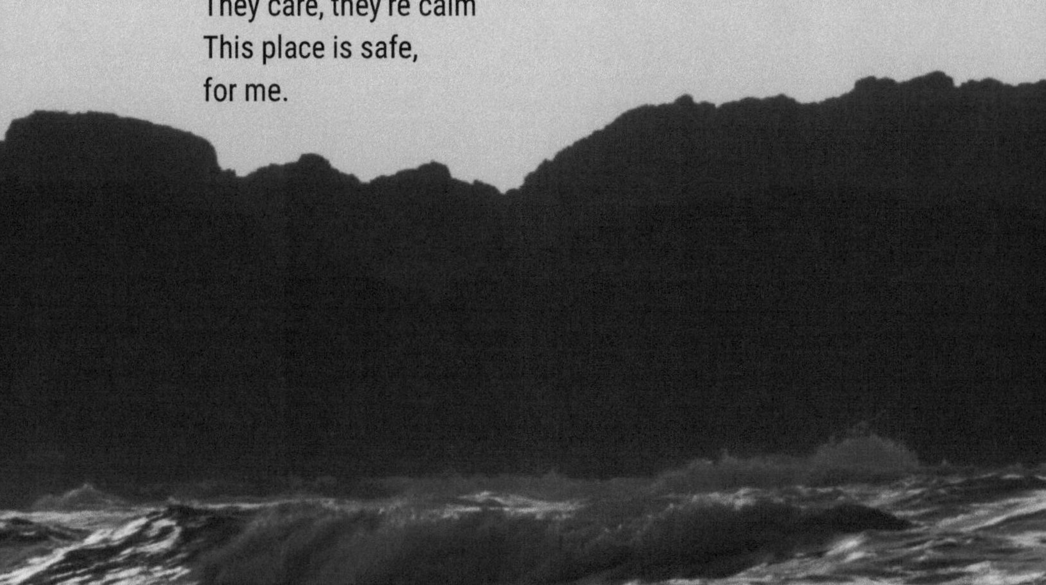

# Brick Wall

I lie crumpled, curled in a ball...
living behind a wall.
Brick by brick it grew
taking away the light of day.
For years I have not seen
the sun of hope rise,
to break the dark surrounding me.

Aching and pleading to the gods
that never hear me scream.
Searching for a way to be free,
carefully, I examine the wall
brick by brick, waiting for the one...
that stands out to me.

Deep red, with a hint of grey.
Desperately, I reach out.
It's raspy to the touch.
I firmly grip the edge,
pushing — pulling.
It will not budge.

Piercing the dark,
I shriek in despair...
but only silence answers me.

Exhausted,
I drop to the ground...
There's nothing left in me.
Cheeks burning...
body trembling.
Emotions filling me.

I listen, trying to catch
what's rumbling inside of me.
"Shame," whispers in my ear.
I shrink to nothing,
as the feeling takes over me.

Staying strong,
I listen to Shame
as it builds inside of me.
Tingling in my hands,
I rub my scars.
Remembering the pain
this emotion has inflicted on me.

Giving space...
Shame abates.
Feeling strong,
I reach out once more.

With a gentle touch the brick moves.
Light breaks through the wall,
exposing the darkness surrounding me.

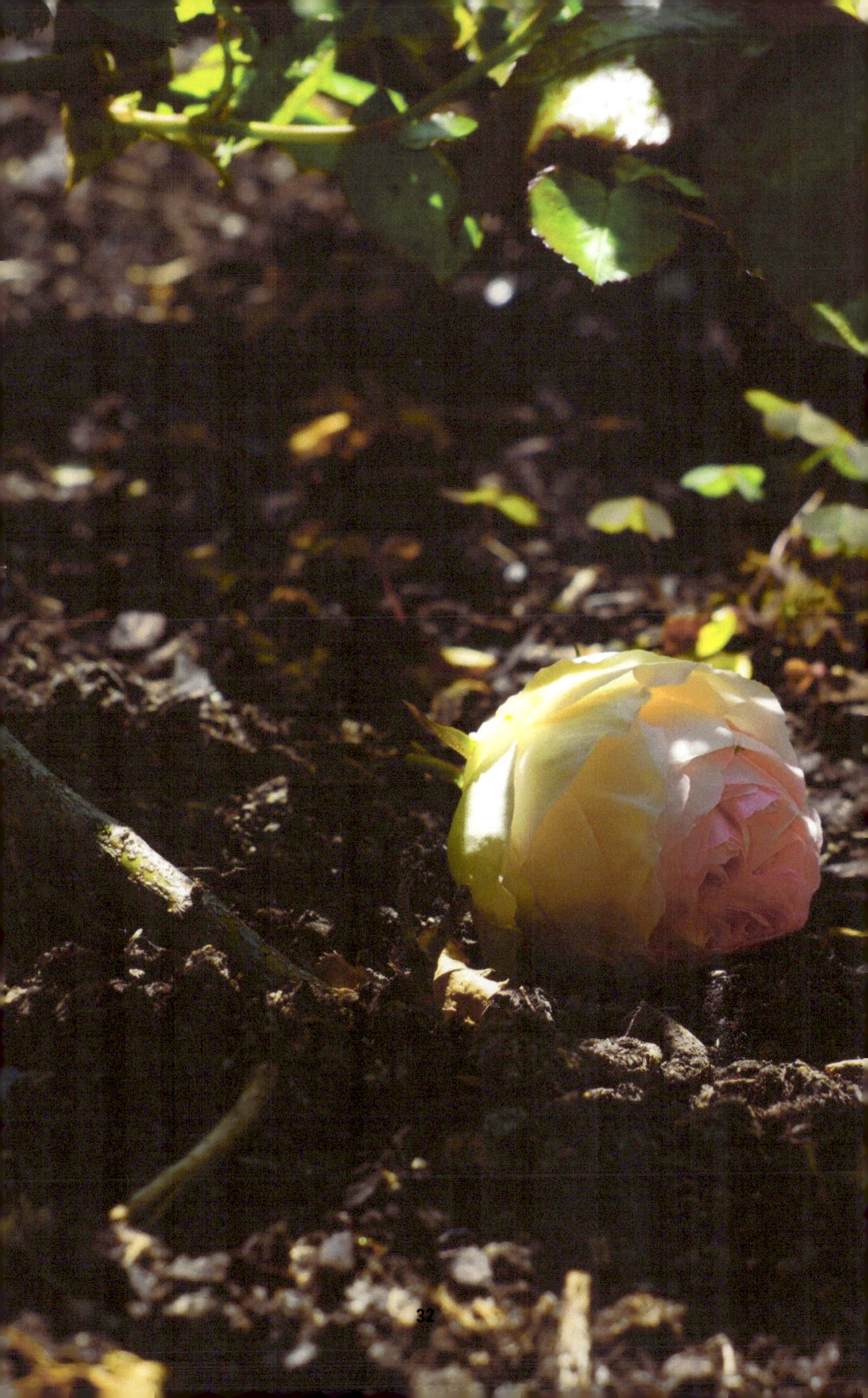

# Broken Warrior

Ready to fight.
You know your strength.

Chin up high,
standing tall,
shoulders strong.

A target of shame
lives on your back.
Beaten for being you.

Your head falls,
shoulders drop.
Your fight to live
abandons you.

Palms clammy,
brow dripping,
airway tight.

All that remains...
A broken warrior,
afraid to fight.

# CALM & CHAOS

# Freedom Inside of Me

Crimson hands slowly grasp my heart.
The enemy has taken hold.

His grip grows tight,
my soul explodes.

> *Breathe in…*
> *breathe out…*

Crying, screaming, I need to run.
No one can set me free.

Thoughts of ending my life,
persuading me.

> *Breathe in…*
> *breathe out…*

No longer can I see hope,
there's nothing left in me.

I must escape,
I cannot live this life anymore.

*Breathe in…*
*breathe out…*

A wave of hope floods over me.
His grip tightens; relief ripped away.

The pain builds once again…
Fear taking hold, filling my veins.

*Breathe in…*
*breathe out…*

His crimson hands, losing strength,
there's nothing more he can take.

His hands slowly…
slipping off my heart.

*Breathe in…*
*breathe out…*

I am free.

# Flash

Smell of fire
fills my lungs.
The orange fiery glow
escapes control.

Fueled by evil in me,
blazing
burning
searing.
Nothing is safe…
near me.

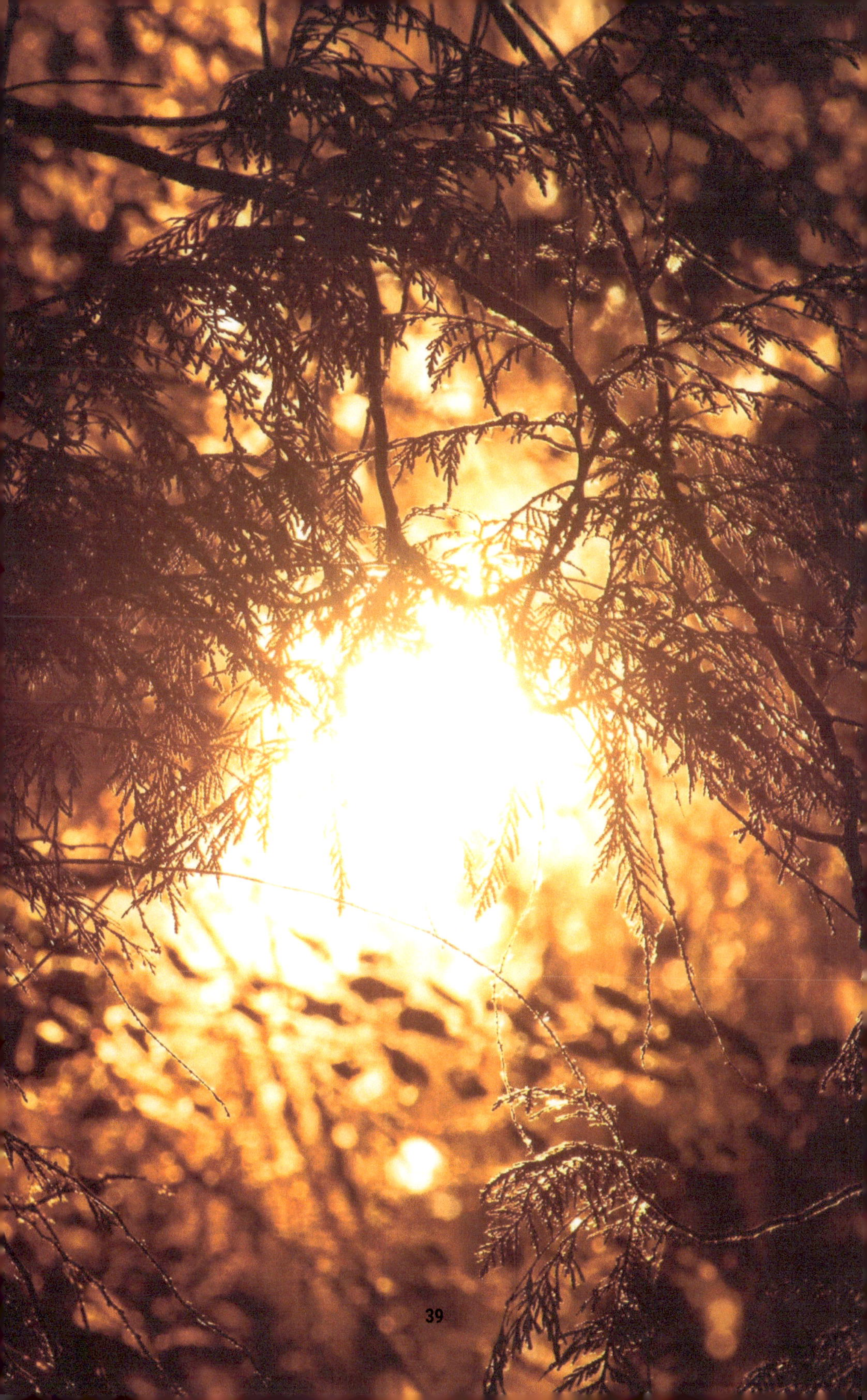

# All I See

Lost in chaos,
reality gone.
The world as others see it,
is leaving piece by piece.
My room disappears,
filling with madness.
Crimson drips from the wall
like shattered eggs.
I try hard to look away,
but am mesmerized by what I see.
Standing on the edge,
of losing my humanity.
My brain shifts,
to the darkest place yet.
All I see is…
murder,
death,
and enemies.

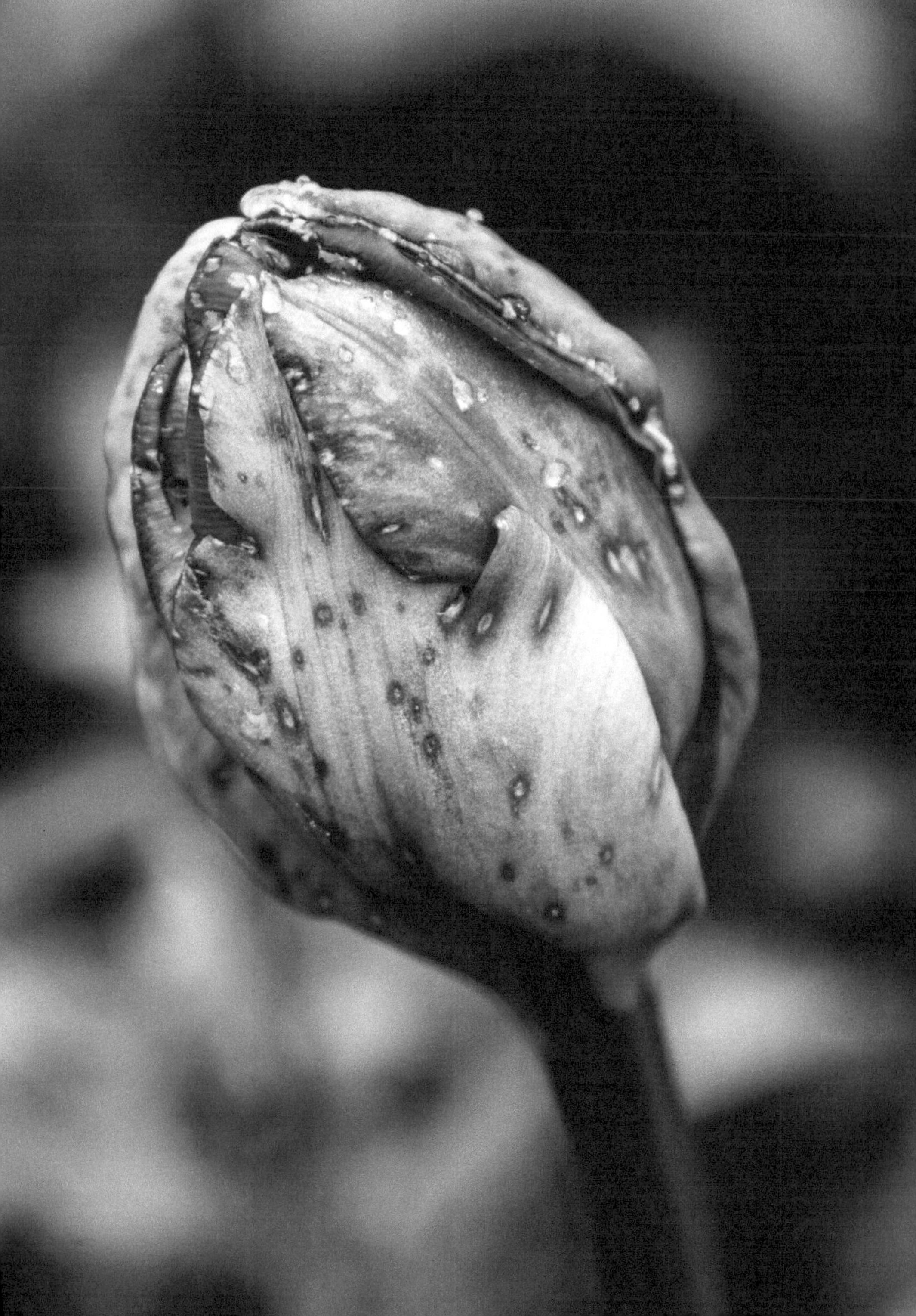

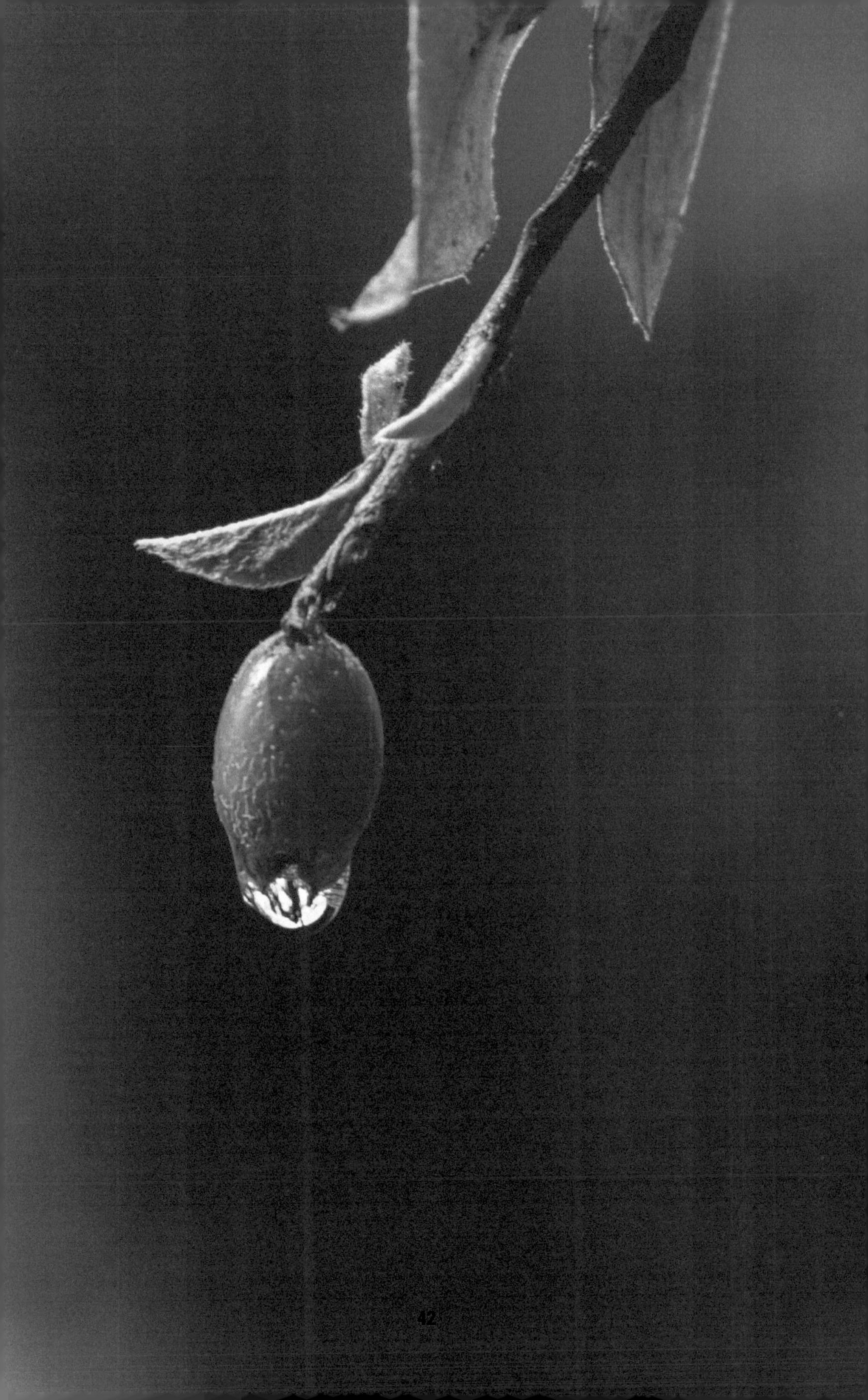

# The Blade

Panic fills my mind,
pain exploding inside of me.
It's been years since
I used the knife.
Yet, the need...
is bursting inside of me.

Grasping the blade.
I feel the edge,
as it softly comforts me.

Gliding smoothly
across my skin
deeper and deeper
with each stroke.

I stop to feel…
the pain and blood,
internal chaos leaving me.
Panicked thoughts now gone,
the deed is done.

I pause…

# Code Blue

I look over to see your ashen face.
I scream - nurses come running to your aide.
"PAU - Code Blue" echoes from above.
You're lying dead next to me.

Everything happening all too fast,
doctors and nurses running to your side,
pounding on your chest, breathing for you.
You moan and groan, as a pulse appears.

You're alive.  Moments ago,
you almost missed seeing your children grow.
Doctors and nurses begin to cheer,
you have made it; you're still here!

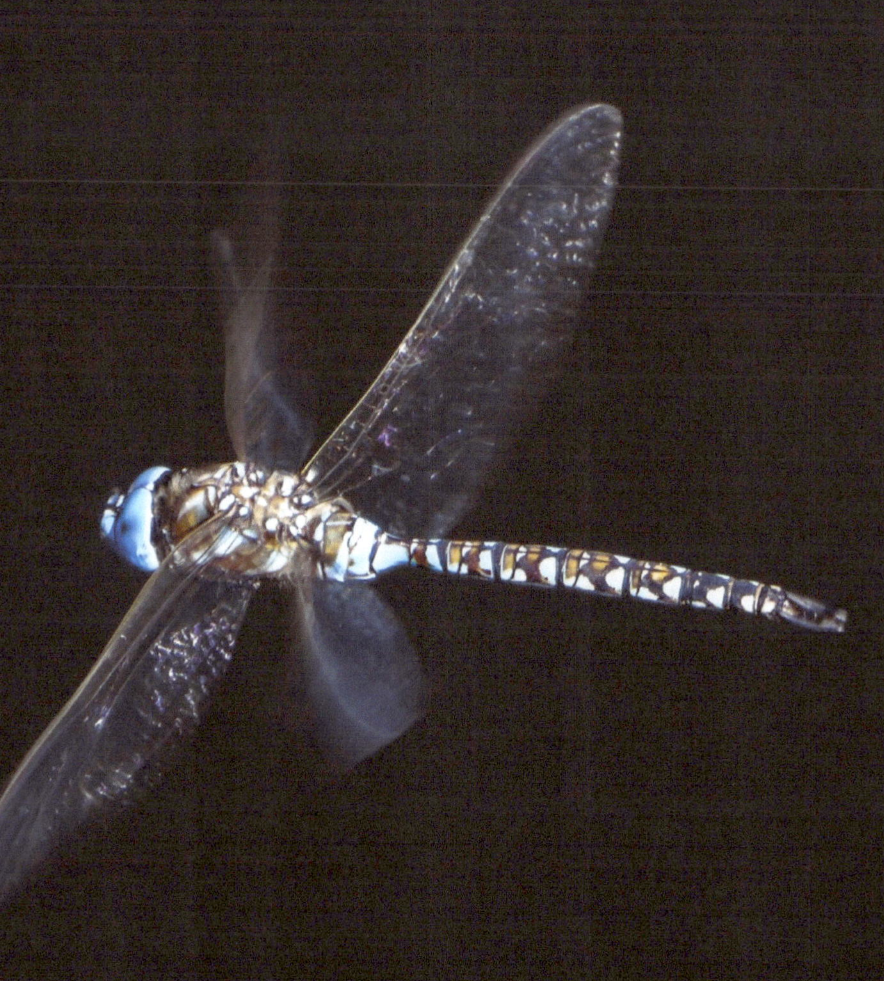

# Impending Doom

Walking along
a tree lined street,
softly singing,
my heart smiling.

Body numb,
skin cold,
sweat dripping.

Trees vanishing
one by one,
Blood draining
from my cheeks.
Gasping for air,
I've lost myself.

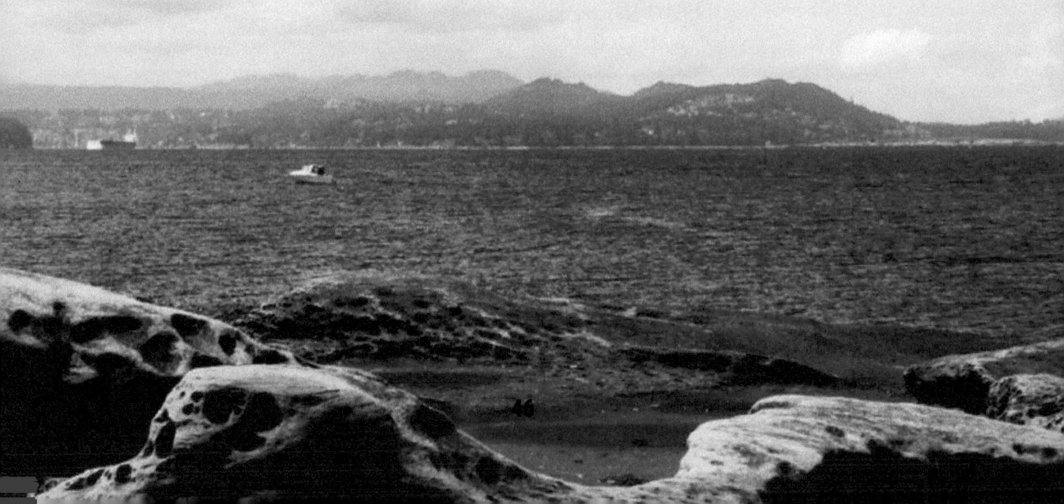

Eyes darting
left and right,
looking for a
place to fall.

Dizziness takes hold.
Collapsing to the ground.
The world is about to end.

I can't explain…
who I am,
or where I've been.

Fumbling to find myself.
Hugging my knees,
shaking…
Impending doom controlling me.

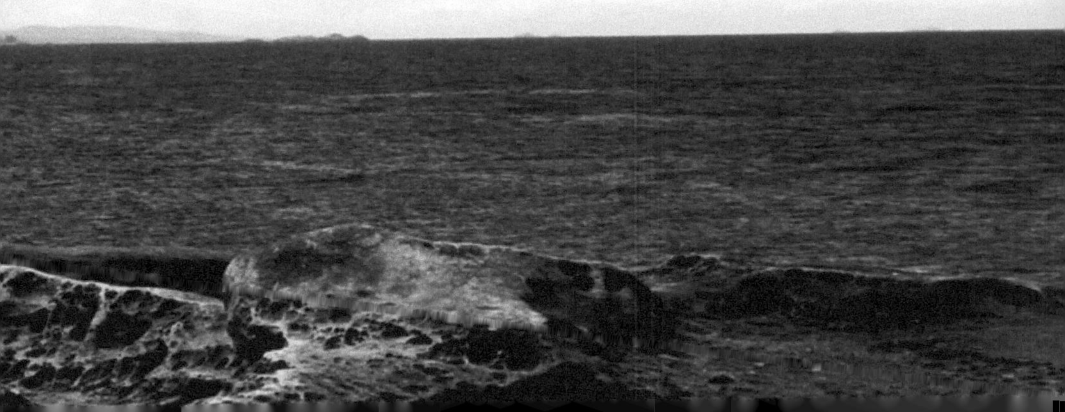

# Normality

Depression changed me...
My heart filled with endless
shame, knowing I'll never be enough...
to live my dreams of sanity.

Meds and therapy
keep me alive.
Day after day I wait,
for a clear mind...

Wishing to be normal,
for a day.

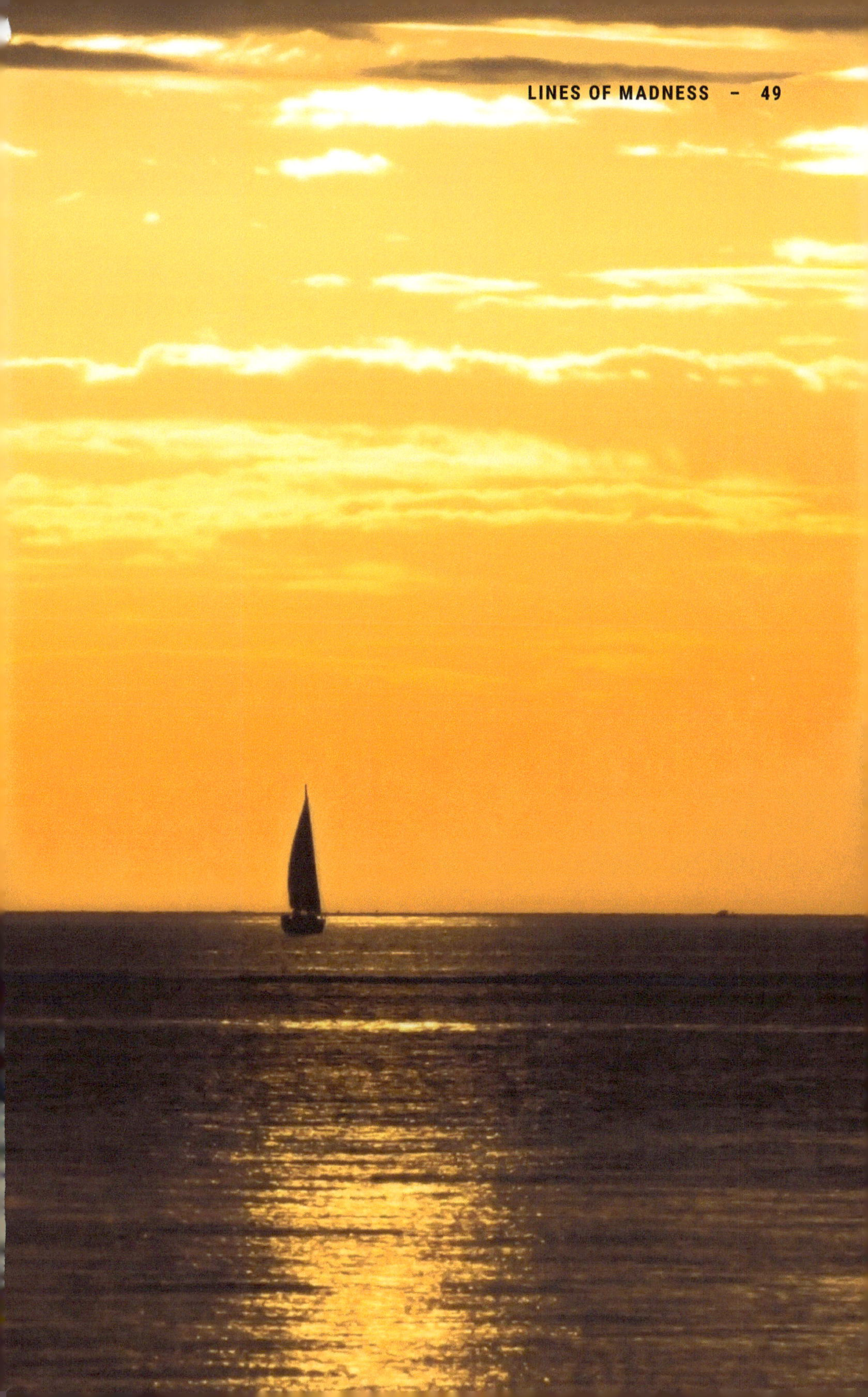

# REALITY & INSANITY

# Friend

No one sees him but me.
Pacing...

> *Forward*
> *Backward*
> *Left and*
> *Right.*

Sitting patiently,
he is watching me.

> *Forward*
> *Backward*
> *Left and*
> *Right.*

I am safe with my friend,
protecting me.

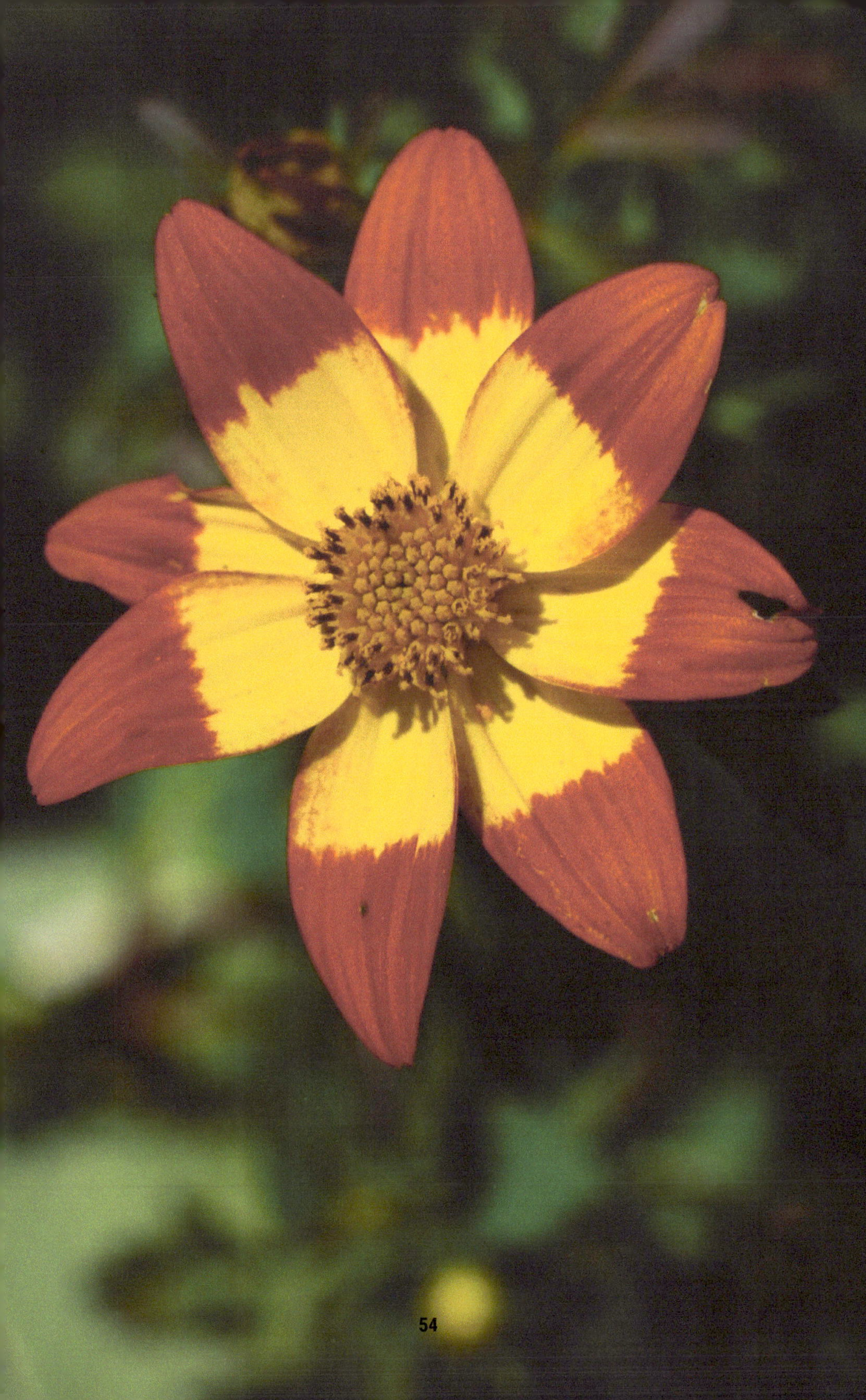

# Tarnished

Cries explode.
Shattering the stillness
enclosing me.

I need my mom.

To see her smile,
to share my dreams
to watch her grow old.

Her life now null.
A darkness
tarnishing me.

# I Can't Fight with You Anymore

There was a girl, screaming at her mom,
yelling the nastiest things.
I saw a boy begging to go home,
wanting to play video games.

I want to be like them.
Can I yell at you?
I want to give you a snotty face!

I want to insist that you are wrong,
and that I am right.

I wish I could hear you say,
'Not right now, maybe later.'
Could we have a fight?

I'd love to hear your thoughts.
To go to a café with you,
laughing and smiling at silly jokes.

Mom,
I wish I could fight with you
one last time.

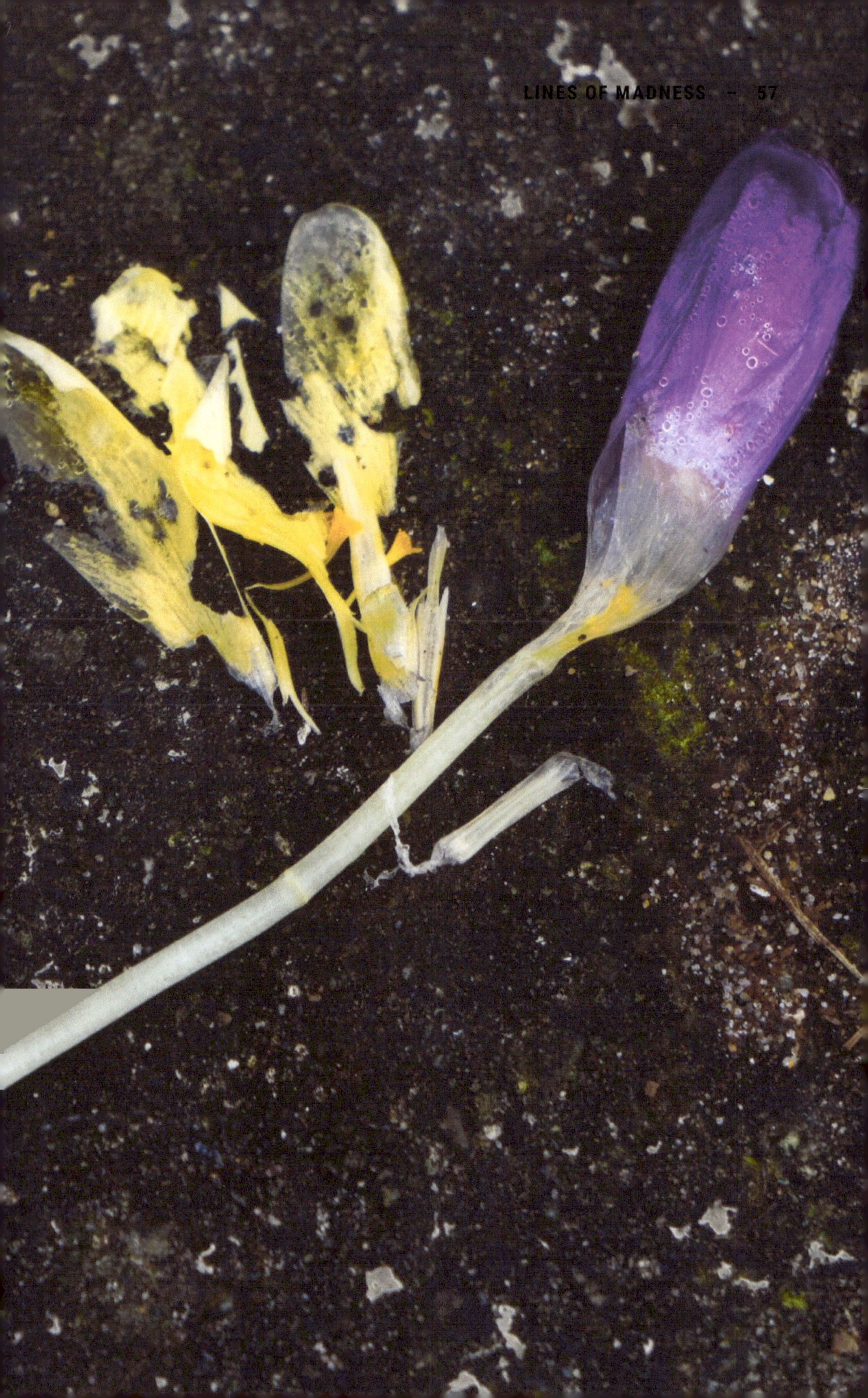

# The End

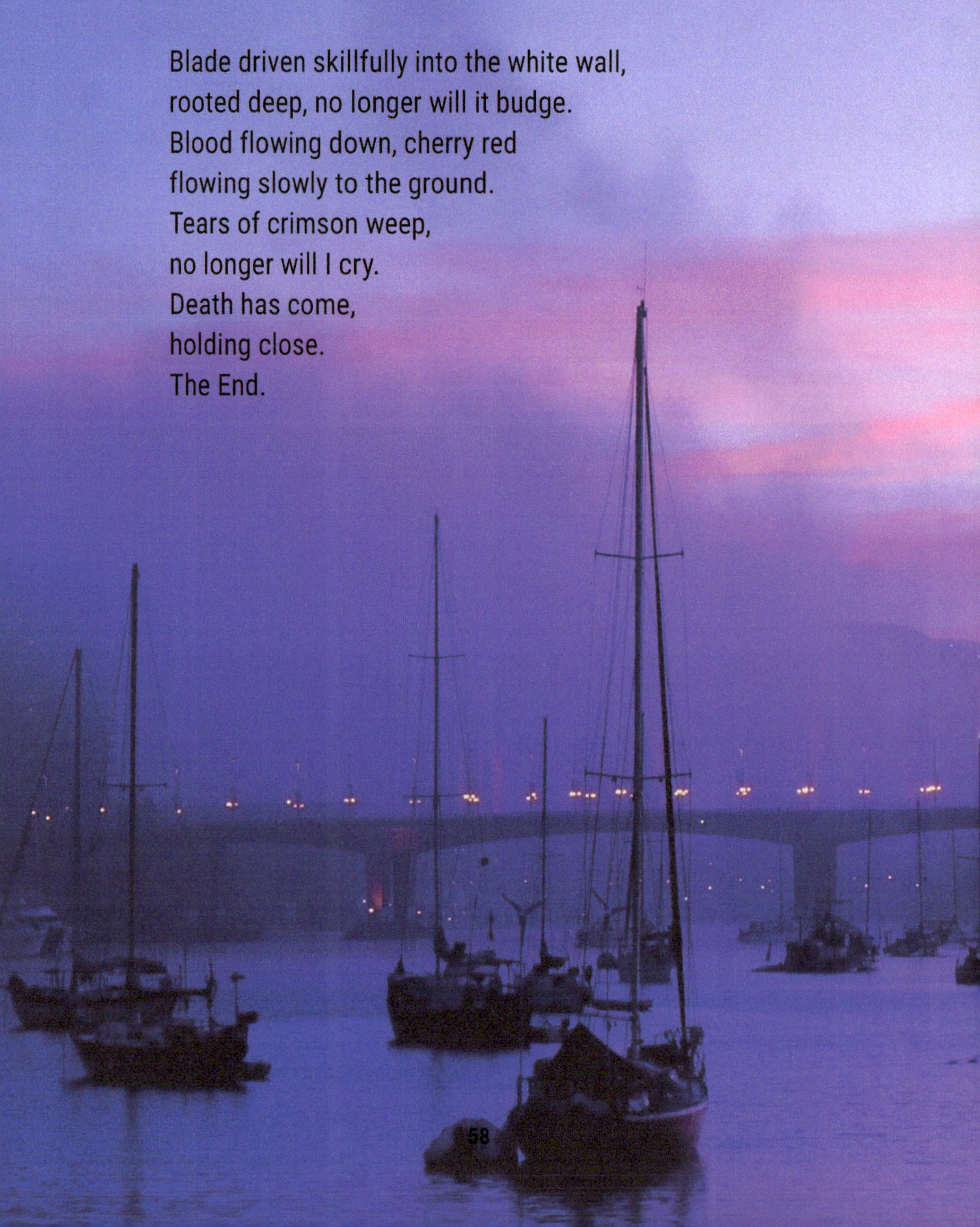

Blade driven skillfully into the white wall,
rooted deep, no longer will it budge.
Blood flowing down, cherry red
flowing slowly to the ground.
Tears of crimson weep,
no longer will I cry.
Death has come,
holding close.
The End.

Eyes feverishly fixed on the sky
desperately wishing I hadn't died

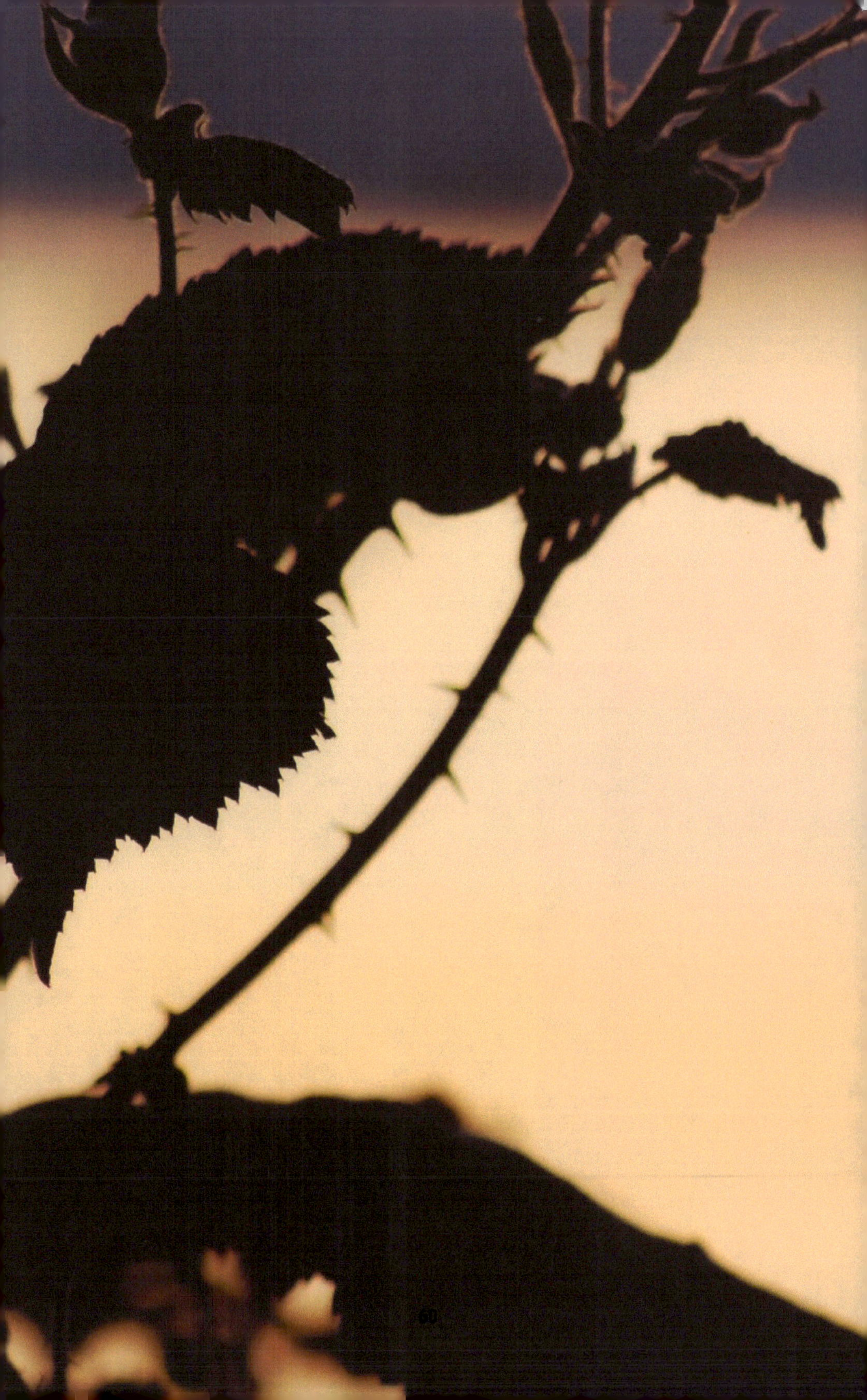

# Perfection

The perfect rose.
Crimson red,
with a subtle glow.

Grasping its stem,
thorns rip through,
blood flows.

Love hurts.
Reach out once more,
loving cautiously.

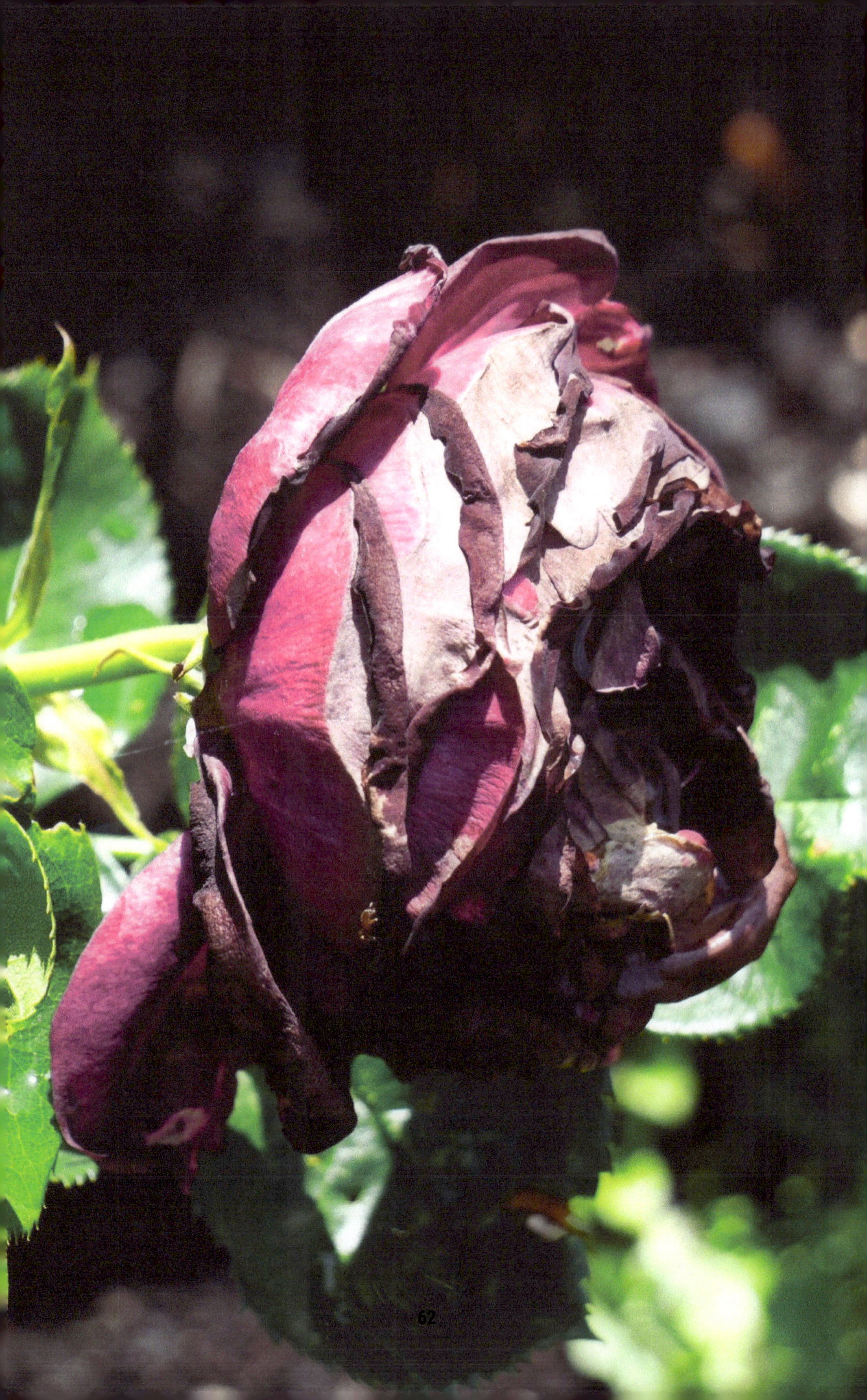

# Betrayal

This morning a stranger asked, who betrayed me the most,
this is how I wish I had answered him…

They held a special place in my heart,
I cared for them even more than myself.
Our connection was unmatched,
we held each other everyday

As time went by, they changed.
Line by line, they tore my skin apart.
I resent them for what they've done,
taking my life away.

It was my Mind,
piece by piece betraying me,
from the inside out, controlling me,
my life and dreams now lost,
depression and psychosis
taking over me.

# The Wall

I place my hand gently on the wall,
I see the blood as it begins to fall.

Thick crimson streaks drip down,
unnervingly fun, like an evil clown.

White walls – stained with red,
lines made with the blood of the dead.

I slowly pull my hand away,
the marks... they fade.  No longer can I play.

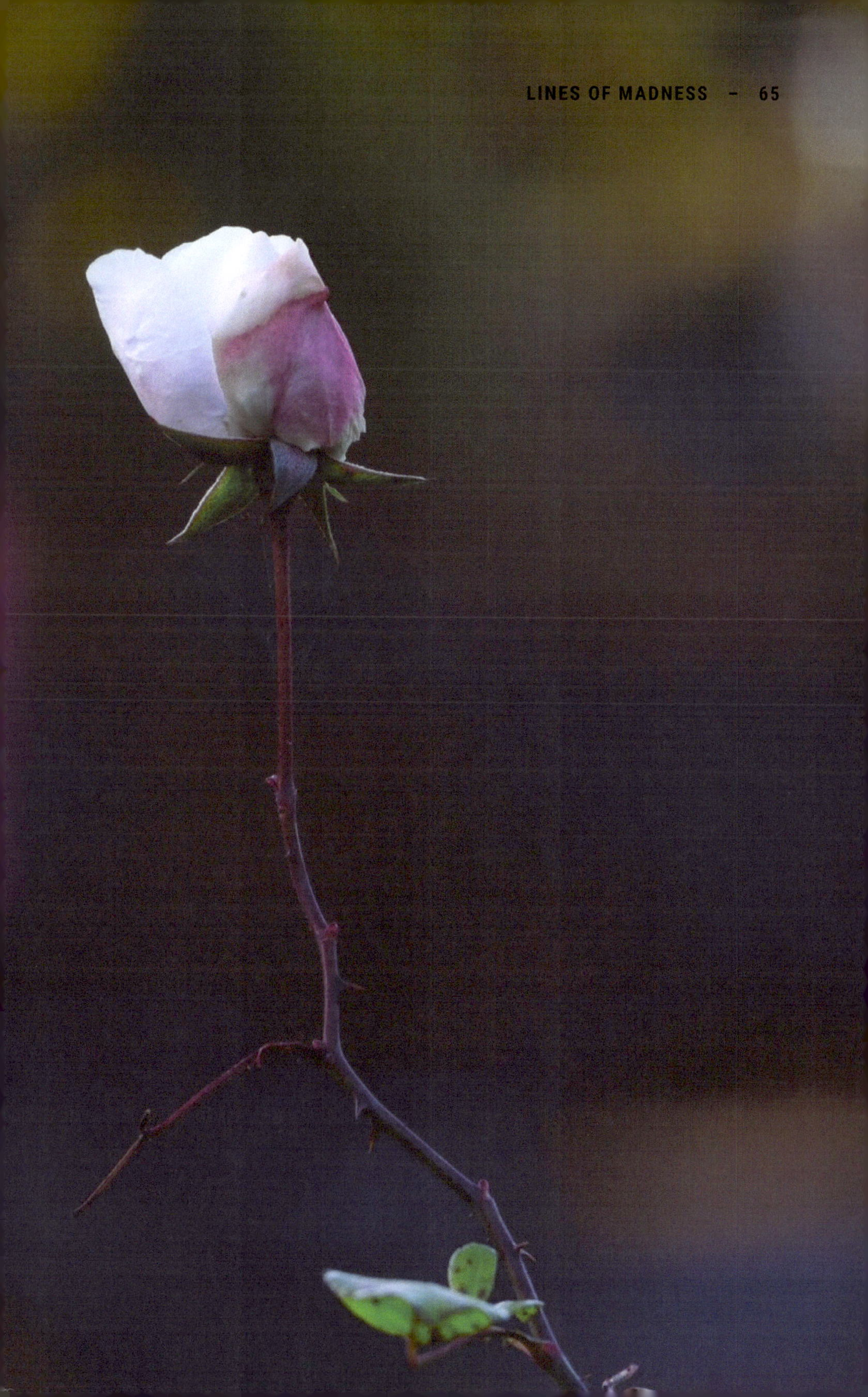

# Suicide

**S**o long ago I felt ok
**U**nited with friends knowing what to say
**I**nch by inch, my soul was torn apart
**C**old engulfs my hands and feet
**I**nside my heartbeat fades away
**D**eath has come to greet me now, the
**E**nd.

# A Writer's Dream

Living a writer's dream,
for hours I write my thoughts.
I have no work, no chores, no life to live.

The catch…
I've been deemed a danger to myself.
I am no longer free,
I don't have my own identity.
Yellow PJs and socks with grips.
I've lost the person I hoped to be,
desperately searching for sanity.

I find solace in staring at the wall.
Hoping one day to see the world
void of deadly tragedies.
No one else sees the blood,
others are afraid of the horrors I see.
Flooded with shame and fear,
I write to cope.

These words,
line by line…
page by page…
express my reality.

# COURAGE & DEFEAT

# My Window

Rocks are thrown,
cracks are made.
The rocks grow larger,
I scream for help.
Bigger and harder
they come at me, I shatter.

Friends come running to my side.
Fix my window, fresh glass
glistens in the sun.

Screams of hate fill the air.
Rocks thrown at me, I shatter.
On the ground I lie,
my window now destroyed.

I cry out once more.
Help comes my way,
Working hard to fix me,
I'm grateful for all they do.

Until, I realize
my window's now
covered by a board.

**Note:** *Found in Diary (Age 14)*

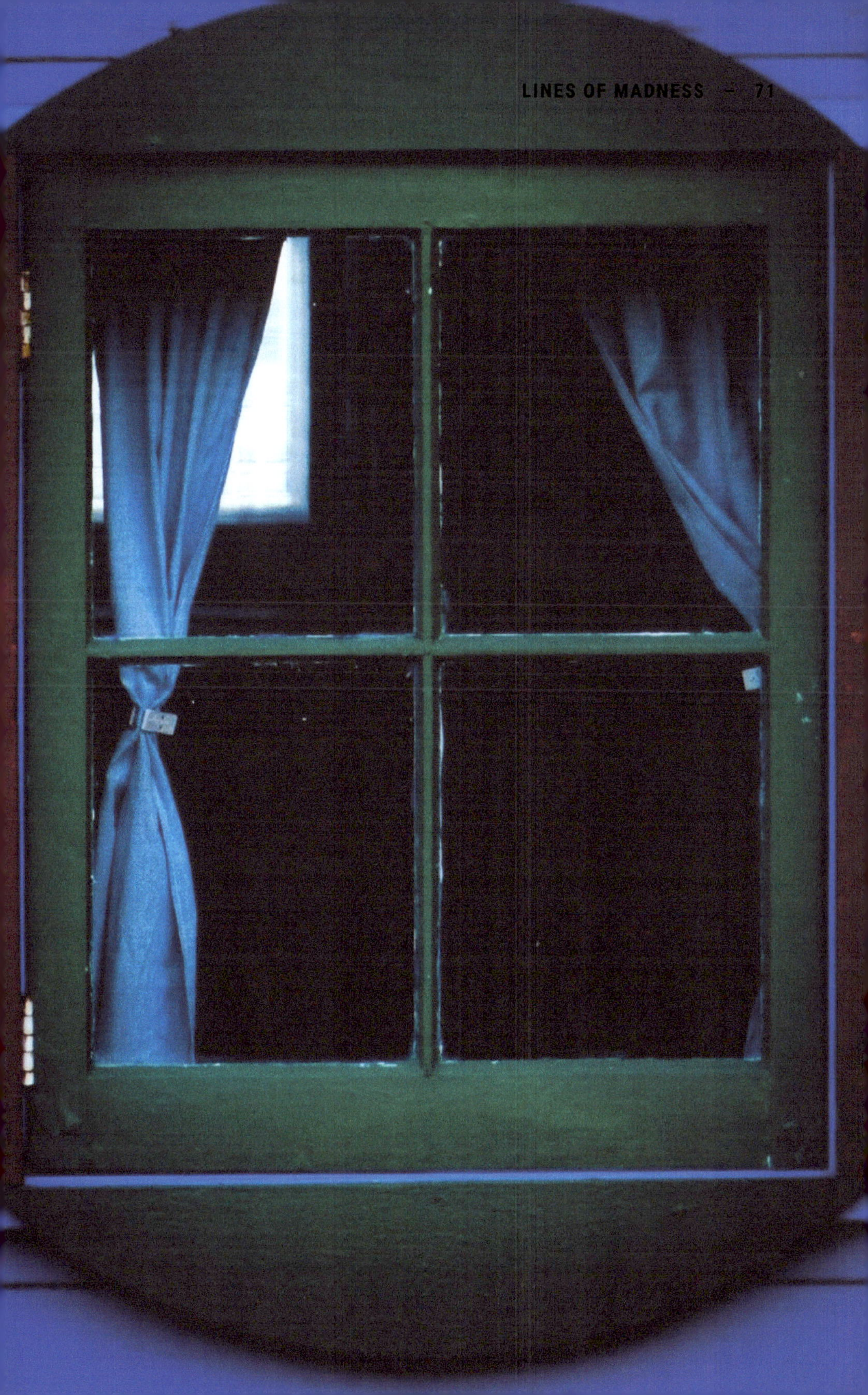

# Different

Morning classes barely done.
Hell begins, your taunting words
piercing through the halls.
You follow me just for fun.

Craftily I lose you.
Fleeing from the world.
I pray no one finds
my safe space
beneath the stairs.

Once I wished to be like you…
to have friends,
to be popular,
to be happy.

But now I see who you really are...
The daggers you throw,
show you are an enemy.

The pain you unleash,
the carnage you leave,
the people you hurt.

My heart
will never be like yours…
My strength will be a voice
for those who feel alone.

I know I'm different than you…
and that's what matters.

Stepping out from the stairs,
I briefly close my eyes...
Remembering to be
proud of who I am.

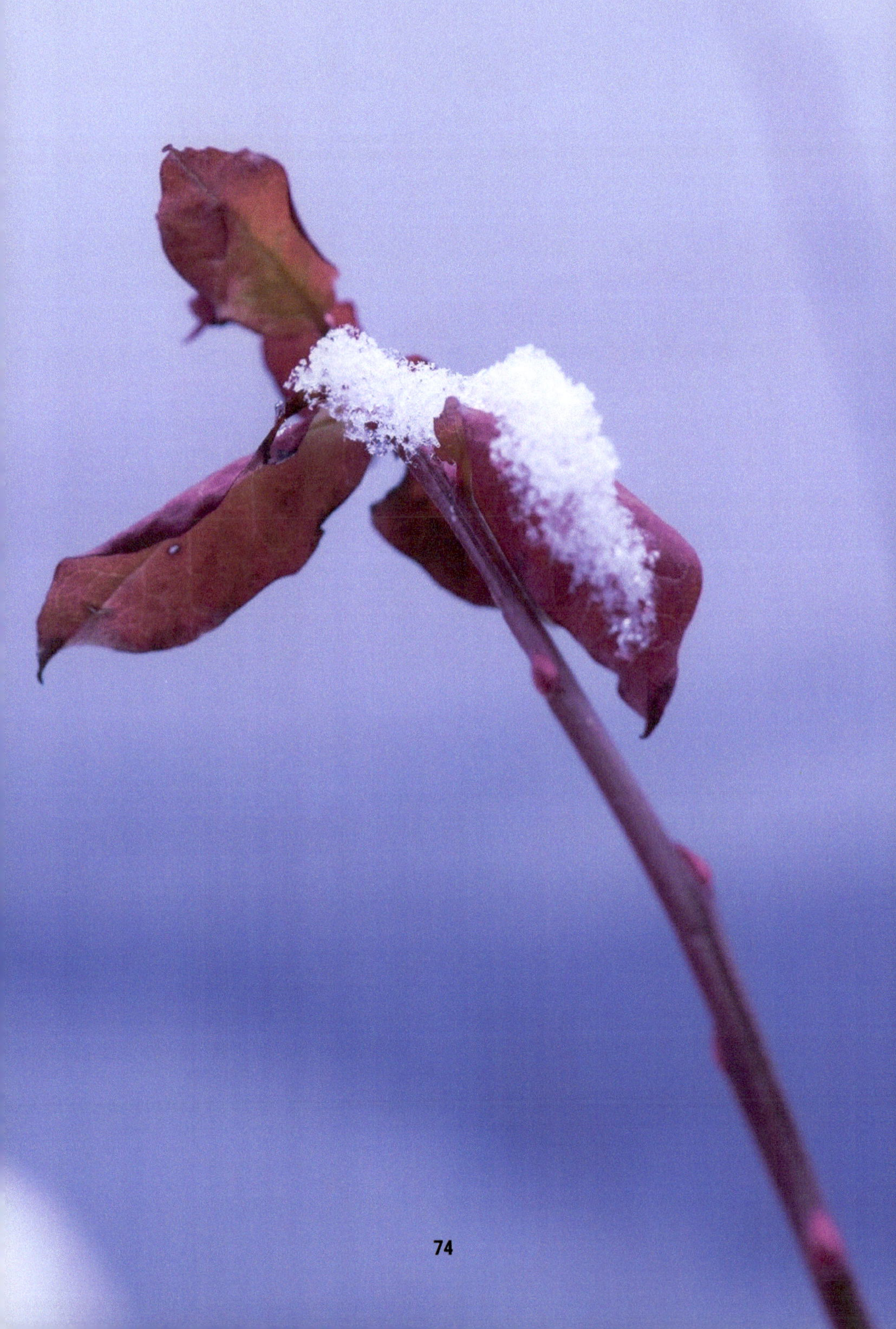

# Defeated

Laying motionless,
aching with doubt,
watching life pass you by.

Your bloodshot eyes
vacantly watch
those you love
continue on.

As you struggle,
alone.

# Change of Trajectory

My chest tightens,
they're talking about me.

*I don't belong here.*
*I belong at home, in my bed.*

My friend pleads,
"they're not ok."
My eyes looking away.
Tears flow like a spring storm.

*My body trembles, my vision shatters.*
*Rubbing my scars, I am not alone.*
*The grooves in my skin, comforting me.*
*Calming the alien living inside of me.*

Tapping his ballpoint pen,
the doctor looks at me and asks,
"Do you understand?"
Shrinking away with each breath.
I hear, "you're staying with us."
Pulling at the cuffs of my sleeves,
no words come...

*When people know what's in my mind,*
*they will run away.*
*My life, my smile, my strength…*
*everything is a façade.*
*"Evil," is how they'll label me.*

The doctor stands up silently
motioning for my friend to leave.
I sob, watching…
as they close door in front of me.

Hours go by.
Slumped over in the chair.
I wake, to laughing outside my door.
Three men come in,
bring me down the corridor,
through two locked doors,
they point to an empty bed.

Staring at the ground,
curled in a ball, I cry.

*Lost, alone, crazy.*
*I'm different now.*

My life has just changed trajectory.

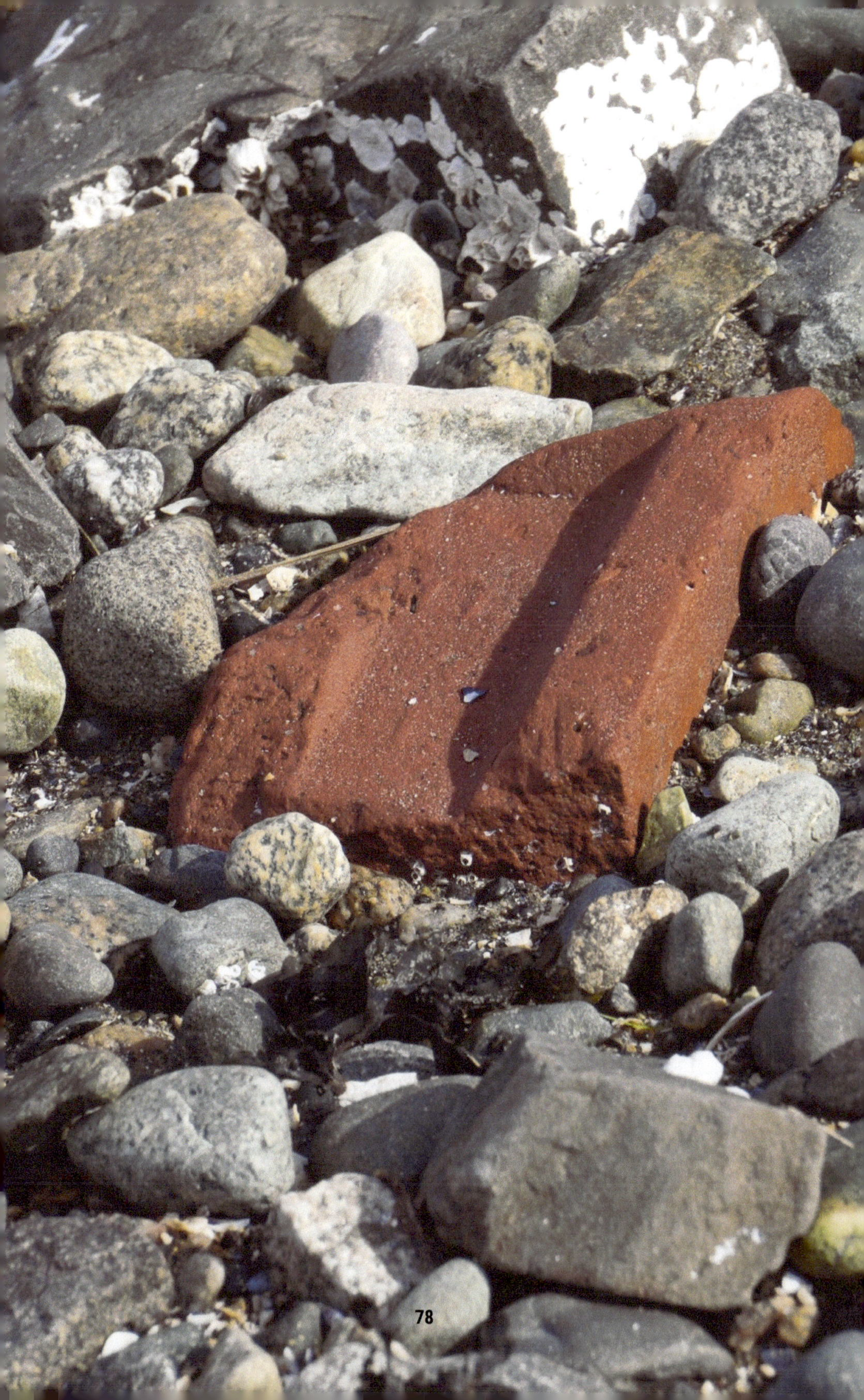

# Walls of Insecurity

I built these walls to keep me safe,
far from hurt and pain.
Holding strong, protecting me
they stood to keep me sane.

The beatings came,
cracks and holes grew large,
but my walls held strong,
through everything.
Until today...

They lost their strength,
crashing onto me.
I lie helpless beneath the rubble.
My insecurities,
crushing me.

# Voices

The voices I hear are so clear,
　　yet others say, silence is all that's near.

Laughing, shouting, and joking about me,
　　yet, no one's really making fun of me.

Screaming and yelling, making themselves known,
　　yet, I'm sitting in this room alone.

They tear me down and throw me out,
　　yet, no one else hears them without any doubt.

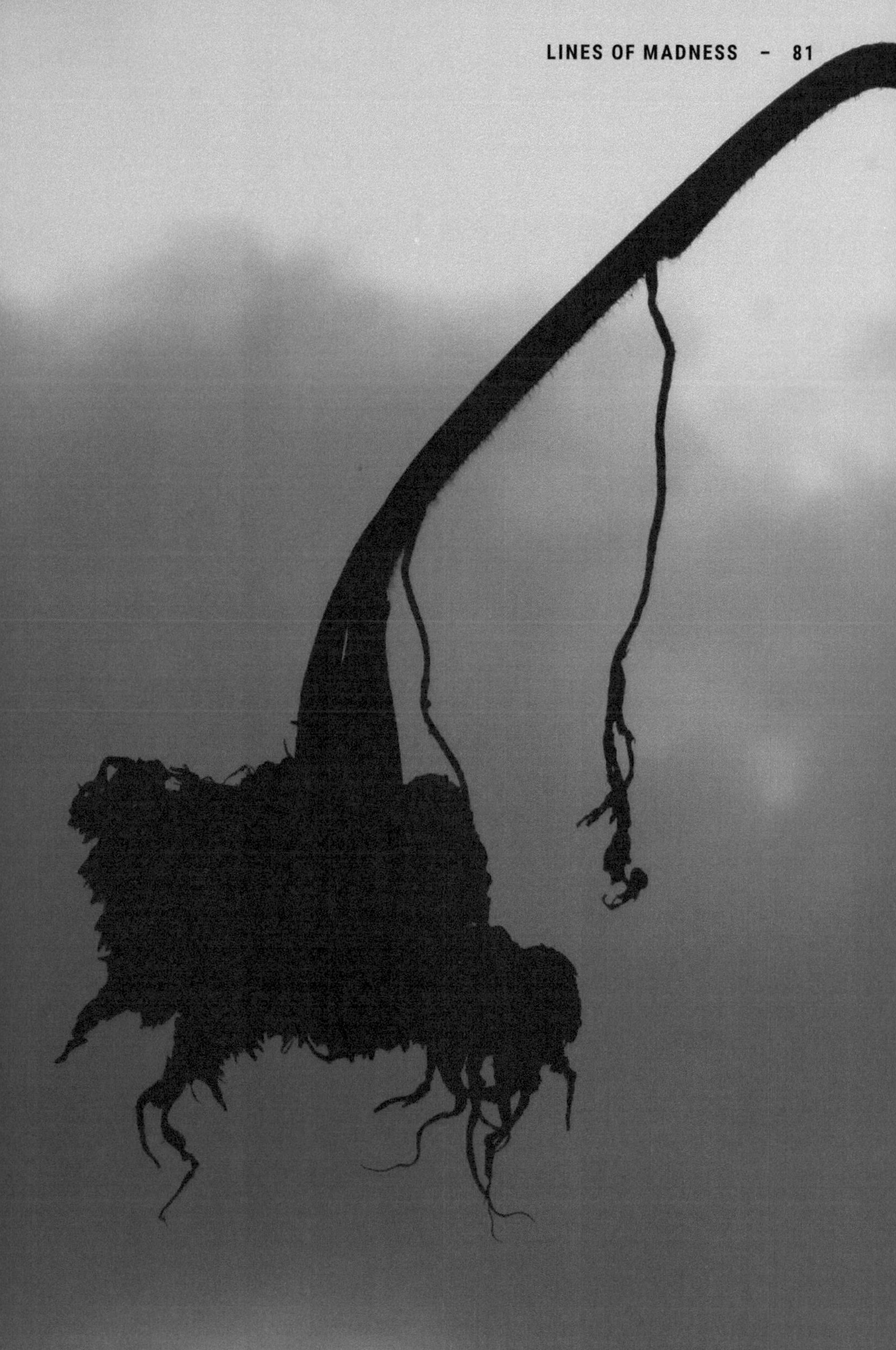

# The Great Escape

Living our days behind locked doors,
wearing yellow PJ's and mesh underwear.
This morning began like the rest.
Dry toast, oatmeal, and an over boiled egg,
spreading jam with a spoon.

We sit and watch the news.
Laughing and joking
about changes in weather,
we will never get to see.

I look up, for a moment,
remembering the feeling of rain
dripping down my cheeks
on a warm summer day.

My stillness shattered
by a piercing squeal,
exploding like thunder
only metres away.

Pushing and pulling on the door,
my friend, begging to be set free.
The door won't budge,
screaming and swearing.

His eyes fixed on the door,
brows furrowed and muscles tightened.
He sprints towards the exit,
crashing hard — it opens, he is free

Frozen,
he is fenced in on all sides.
Not a moment wasted.
He jumps over the gate.
He is free.

Sitting and watching the news alone.
I think about my friend,
hoping that he is truly free.
But knowing deep inside
that he won't be hard to find,
running through the world
wearing yellow PJs and mesh underwear.

***Epilogue:***
    *Three hours later...*
    *Screams and shouts echo through the halls,*
    *pleading for them to let him free.*
    *Escorted by 5 men,*
    *They force him into solitary.*
    *Holding him down, they inject him…*
    *Silence fills the ward,*
    *he's back, now locked behind blue doors,*
    *still wearing yellow PJs and mesh underwear.*

# Death on my Doorstep

Death is here... a shadow,
peeking through frosted glass.
Waiting for my door to unlatch.
I watch his every move.
Soon, he slips out of view.

I slide my door, just a crack.
This is it, he takes his chance.

Screaming – slamming the door.
I try to keep him out,
but he fights his way into me.
Calmness sucked out of me.

Looking down I see a knife,
Terrified, wondering if this is the end.
Pain engulfs, chest tight.
Redness flows from my arms and legs.

My body frozen – blood runs free.
Pain so strong, I cannot feel.
Numbness taking hold of me.
Lines of red cover my pale skin.

My hand holding the knife.
This cannot be
Death took control of me.
Tears flowing down my cheeks.

I breathe in and out,
determined to be set free.
This is a fight inside of me,
cracking my knuckles.

I'm ready to end
Death's hold on me.
Standing strong
I remember who I am.

Death screams and cries.
feelings of love and hope
forcing his lies out of me.
Joy and hope growing.

Building a wall of strength,
he cannot cross.
I throw him out of me.
Hands spasming, head shaking,
he runs away. Door latched.
I am safe, for today.

# INNOCENCE & PAIN

# The Nursery

Late one Friday night,
I was told there was a way for
Jesus to set me free.
All I had to do was to come to the nursery,
and we'd pray the demons away.

Wearing my favourite red hoodie…
Bible in hand, bubbling inside,
excited that God would end my pain.

They told me to lie on the floor.
In the name of God
both arms and legs pinned down,
to stop me from getting away.

Screaming in fear, I could not move.
They claimed each scream
were the demons leaving me.

Speaking in tongues,
my chest beaten by the Bible in their hands,
claiming freedom from
demons of self-harm and suicidality.

Shaking in terror… crying…
begging them to let me free.
No one suspected the torture
that was happening in the
Children's Nursery.

Weakened after over an hour of fight…
I gave up, nothing left inside.
My body a heavy weight,
I could not move.
Exhausted, on the floor,
letting them leave bruises on me.

In my stillness,
they looked at one another,
nodded and praised God for saving me.
Letting me go, they declared,
that Jesus set me free.

The children's space of play,
was just witness
to innocence being snatched away.

No longer would I be the same.
My trust in humans and God, gone.
I am forever tainted
by this memory.

# Lost

Volcanoes rupture,
burning…
consuming…
my memories.

My life burnt away…
my mind stolen.
No longer can I find
the person I was
before that fateful day.

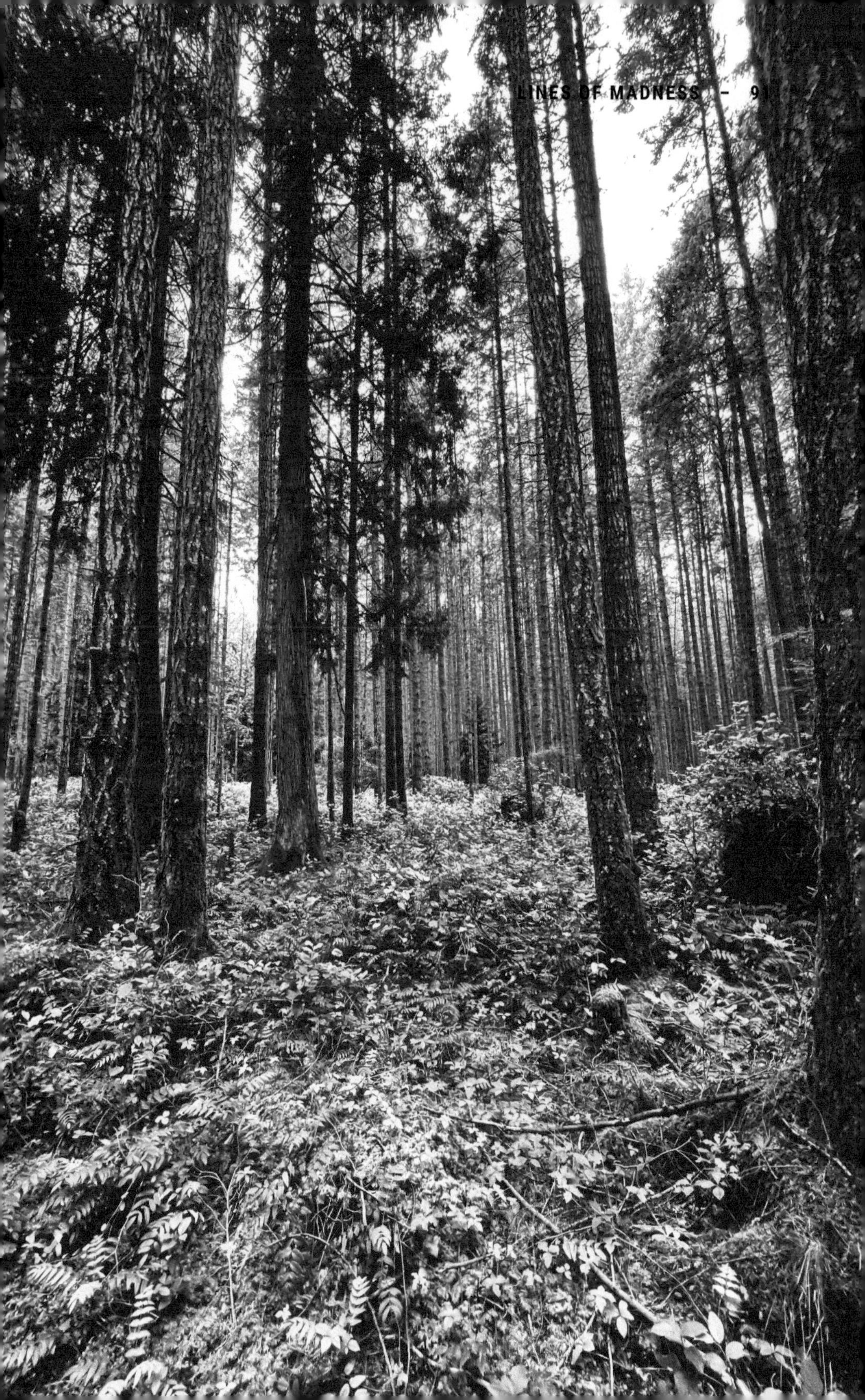

# The Crayon

Frustration fills the air,
like the smell of a burnt birthday cake.
I hear a blaring scream,
"There must have been a mistake!"

Looking up, I see him pleading desperately.
Claiming he didn't mean to throw
the crayon at the nurse's head.
He is frantically begging to be let free

Sitting quietly I try to look away, but
His eyes latch onto me. I pray,
"Please make him stop
coming over this way."

Hands shaking,
no longer can I see the words
trembling on my page.
I force my eyes into my book,
pretending like he is far away.
Eyes fixed on my chest he asks,
"Can I feel, just this once?"

My heart cringes,
remembering a man from long ago.
My body forced to do
what what no one can explain.

This man taught me that
my body was never mine.
I am merely a man's doll
with a vagina and breasts as anatomy.
Obedience was how I survived,
it hurt less than when I'd fight.

Remembering those days, I stop.
It's time to take a stand.
This man in front of me,
will not take advantage of me.
Now is the time, to stand up for me.

I look him in the eyes.
Redness grows on my chest and face.
Trembling, I reach for a crayon.
With perfect aim I hit him on the nose,
"Sorry, I didn't mean to throw
that crayon at your face."

My feet planted, ready for a fight…
I look him in the eyes,
turn and walk away…
knowing that this prick
isn't worth my energy.

# Pain

Pain seeps from your eyes,
burning like acid
rolling down your cheeks.

Your voice muted,
pleading for someone
to believe in you.

Red lines etched
each tear leaving their mark.
Alone, killing you.

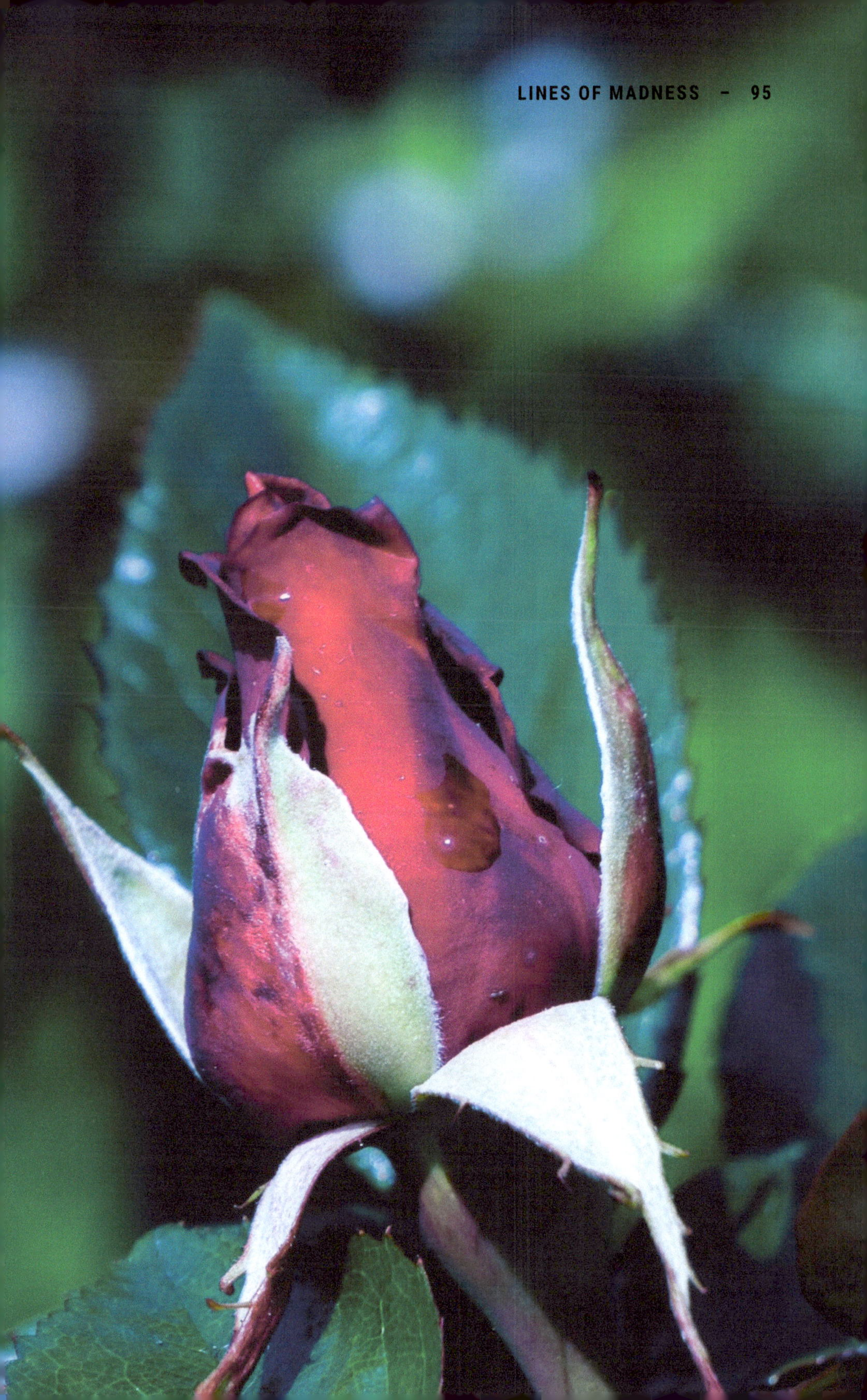

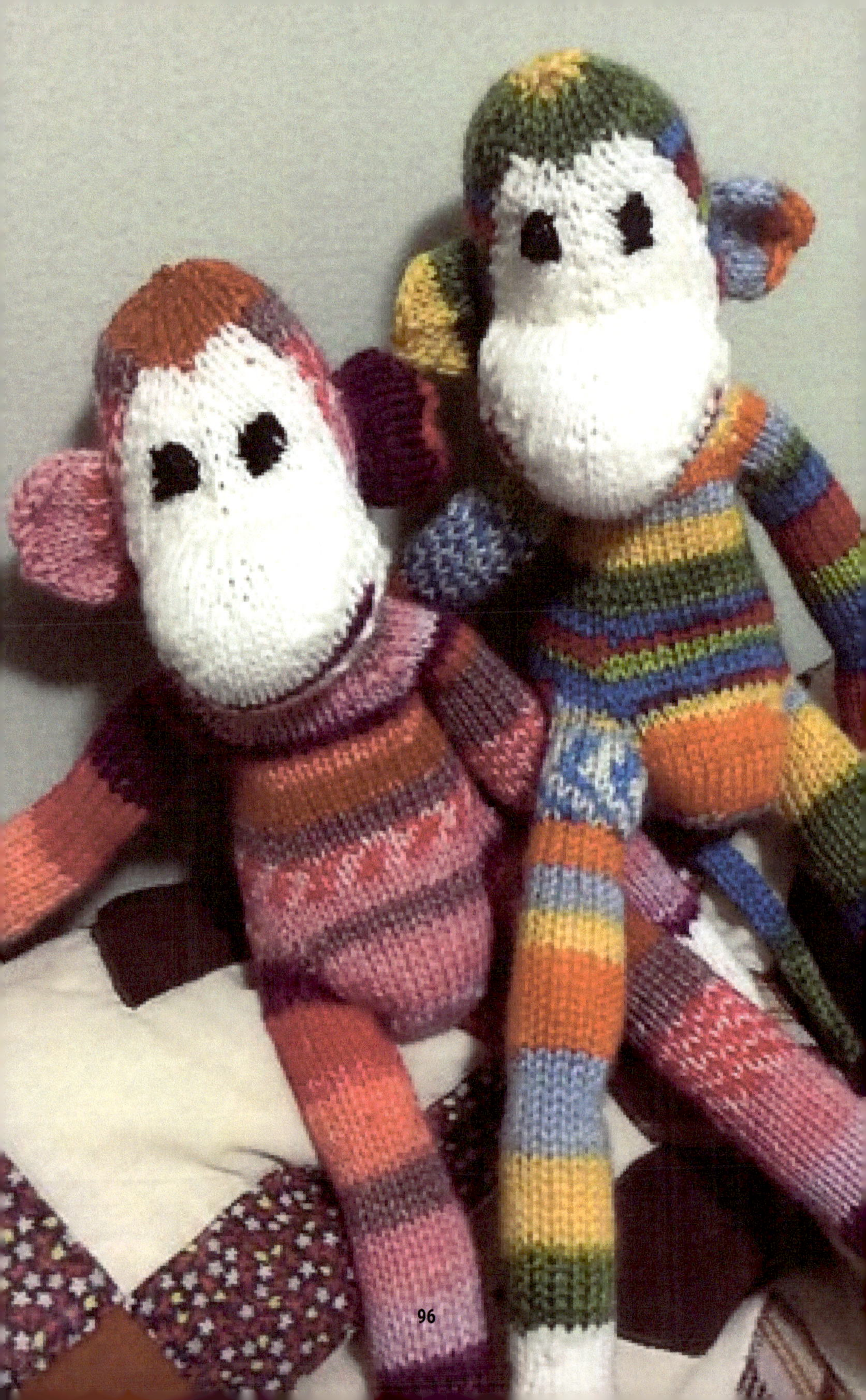

# Teddy

Feeling lost deep inside,
I need someone to hear…
my pain, my cries.

I know I need my life to end.
I scream out loud with all my might,
"Please Teddy…
let me die!"

I look into Teddy's button eyes,
he looks away.
Tears rolling down his cheeks
shaking, he covers his face.

"What's wrong?" I ask.
"Don't leave me now,
my dear friend,"
chin trembling, he continues on,
"Your life means so much to me,
it does not need to end."

Speechless, my body tingling…
my death would leave
a life in disarray.

# 6 Years Ago

6 years ago, I lost you.
I didn't lose your love,
but I lost your hugs.

I whispered in your ear,
that we'd be ok,
within seconds you left your pain.

I saw you breathe your last,
but I don't remember
why it wasn't like the rest.

I whispered,
'Dad, I think she's gone.'
I wish I'd been wrong.

Dad cried into the wall, 'Why?'
No words could answer.
I called your son, 'Mom just died,'
silence was all I heard.

I couldn't tell your daughter.
But, she had to know.
I told Dad, that I couldn't ruin her life too.
He told her that the world had let you go.

I said goodbye,
but I'm not sure if I did it right.
I looked at your body and waved,
forgetting that your eyes were shut tight.

I looked back once again,
hoping your death was a lie.
It couldn't be my mom,
lying frozen having died.

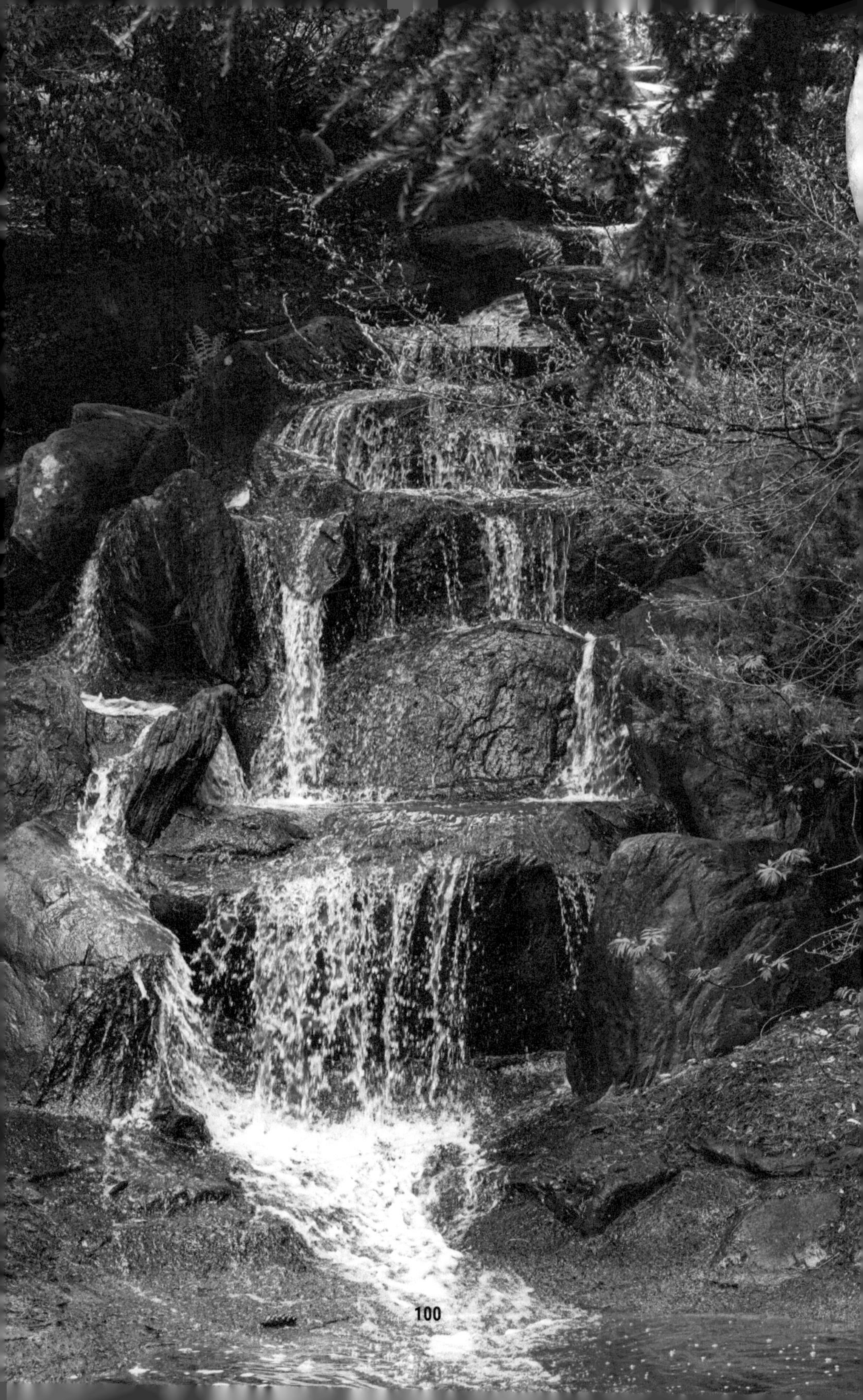

# Tears

Crimson tears
flow down my leg.
Each drop a reminder that…
That I exist.

Exposing what's inside of me…
my pain,
my loss,
my suffering.

My life, etched into my skin,
fragile like a frozen waterfall.
One day, I will have
the strength to let go.

To live a life,
where tears of blood
no longer need to flow.

# Nameless

Lost, without a name.
There's no one to call
who feels the same.

Each light you have on earth
sheds a shadow of protection
from pain and hurt.

Loss sears my heart,
I am lost without a name,
with nowhere to start.

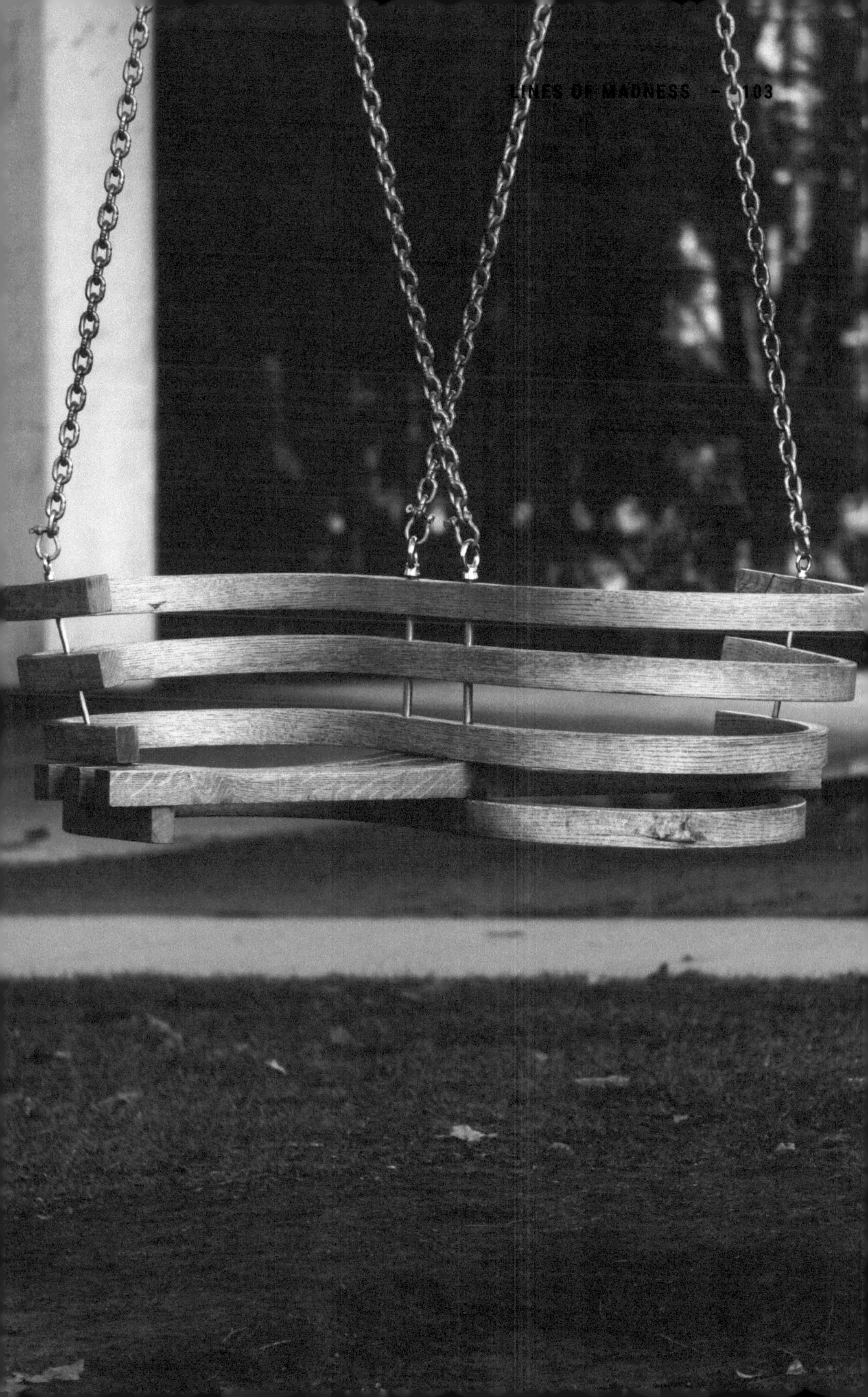

# Heart

My beating core of emotions,
frozen by my own insanity.

Dizziness takes over
as agony radiates in my chest.

Blood no longer flowing,
darkness settles in my veins.

No strength left inside,
without my heart, I will die.

Moment by moment,
my feelings are named.

Beat by beat I move my soul,
letting my emotions grow.

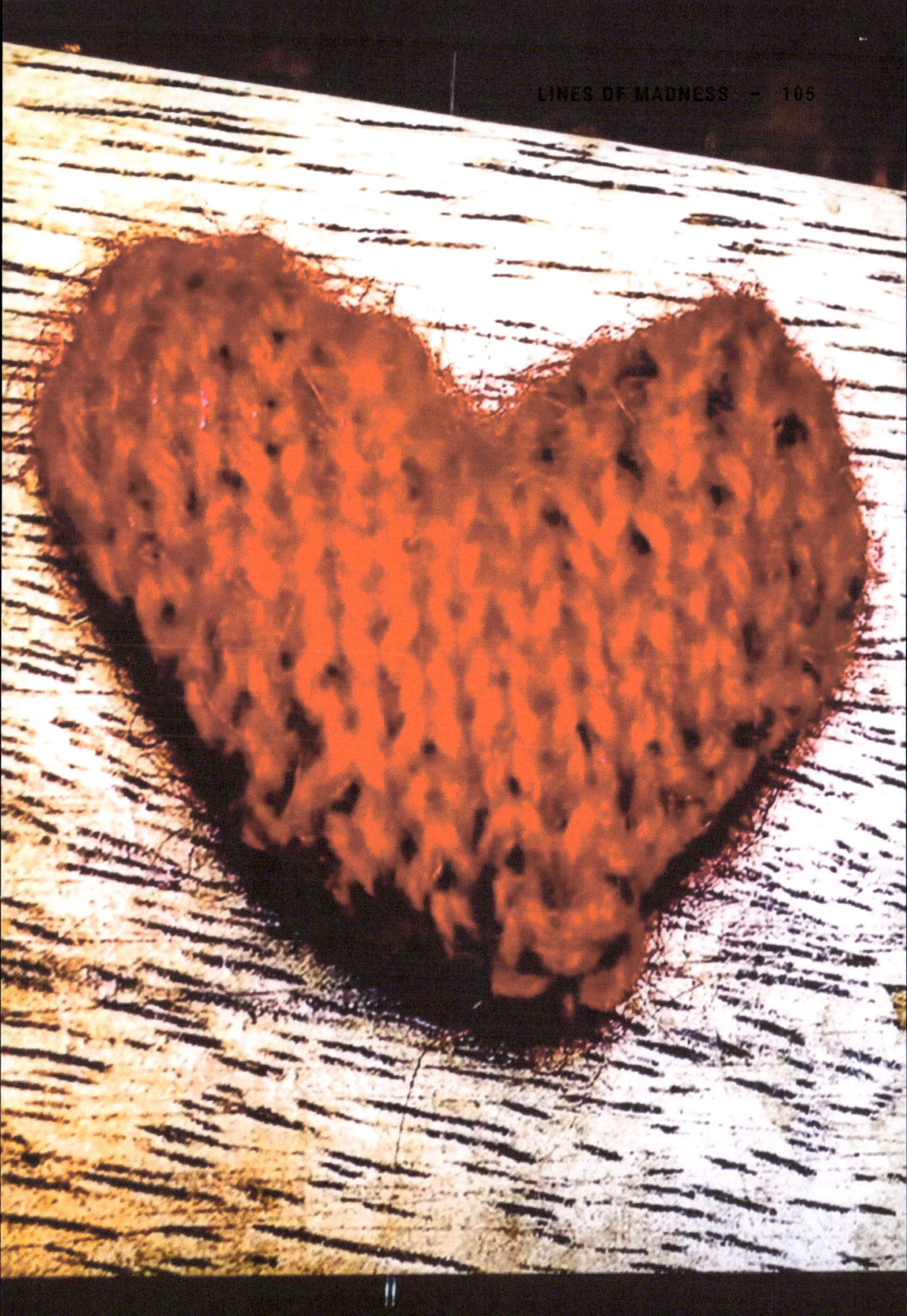

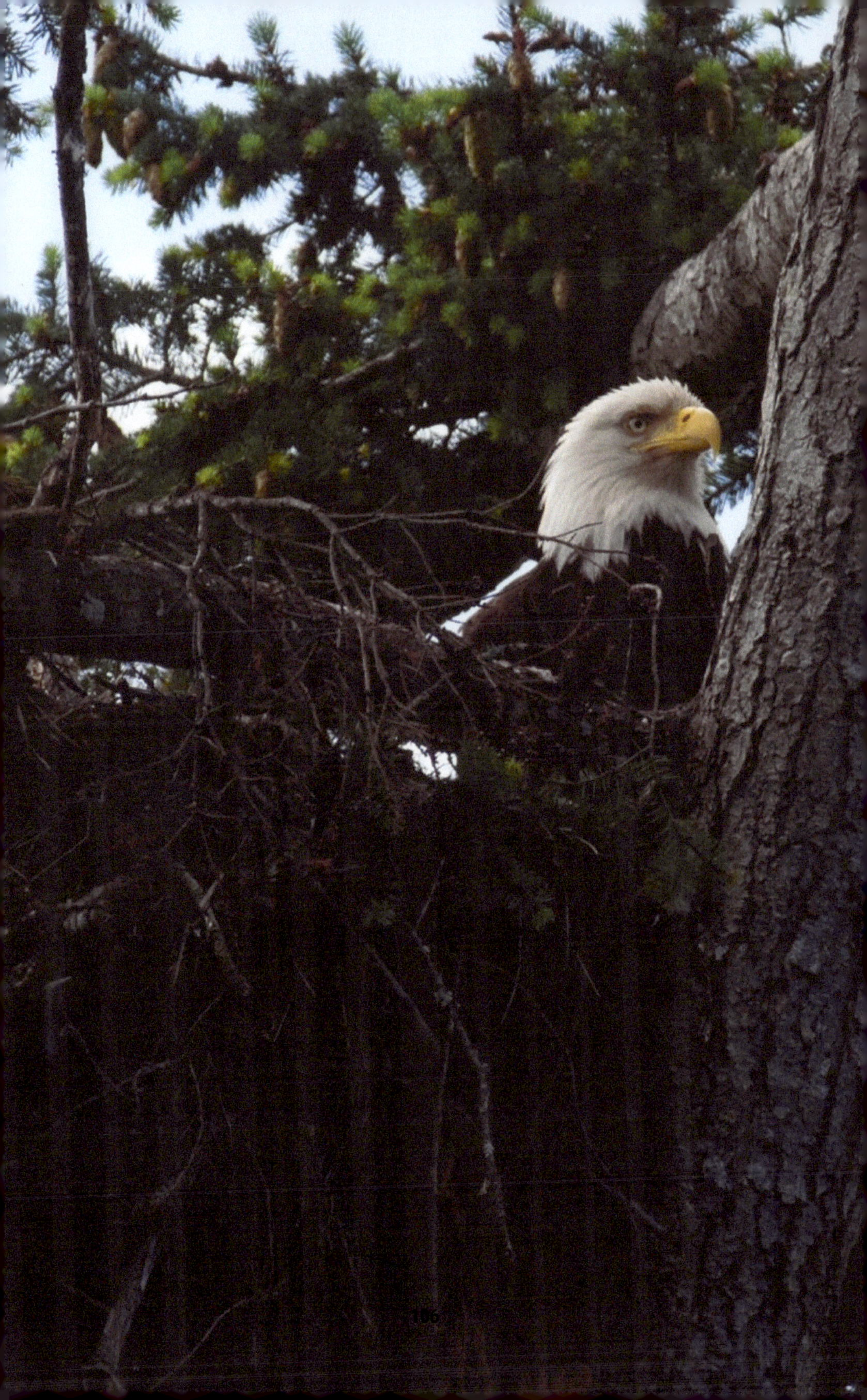

# Fire

Scraping through the rubble,
my life burnt to ashes.
I find a child hurt,
crying – covered in burns.
Collapsing to the ground.

I recognize her eyes, she is me.
Unknown to me, this child
has been in my fire for years,
battling my hurt, my pain.
Fighting to keep me safe.

Tears in my eyes,
I pick her up and bring her near,
reminding her it's safe to rest,
thanking her for all she's done.

# AWARENESS & NUMBNESS

# Emotions of Me

Sadness,
      a spring river flooding my eyes.
Fear,
      suffocation like boa constrictor strangling me.
Pride,
      bubbling brightly like a rainbow in the sky.
Shock,
      a waterfall frozen in time.
Depression,
      pain engulfing me, like a tornado as it lands.
Hope,
      reaching out with a mother's secret remedy.
Regret,
      beating me, like I'm in a fighting ring.
Love,
      jumping inside, like an bunny ready to play.
Jealousy,
      fills my cheeks, burning red with fire.
Vulnerability,
      sharing Lines of Madness with You.

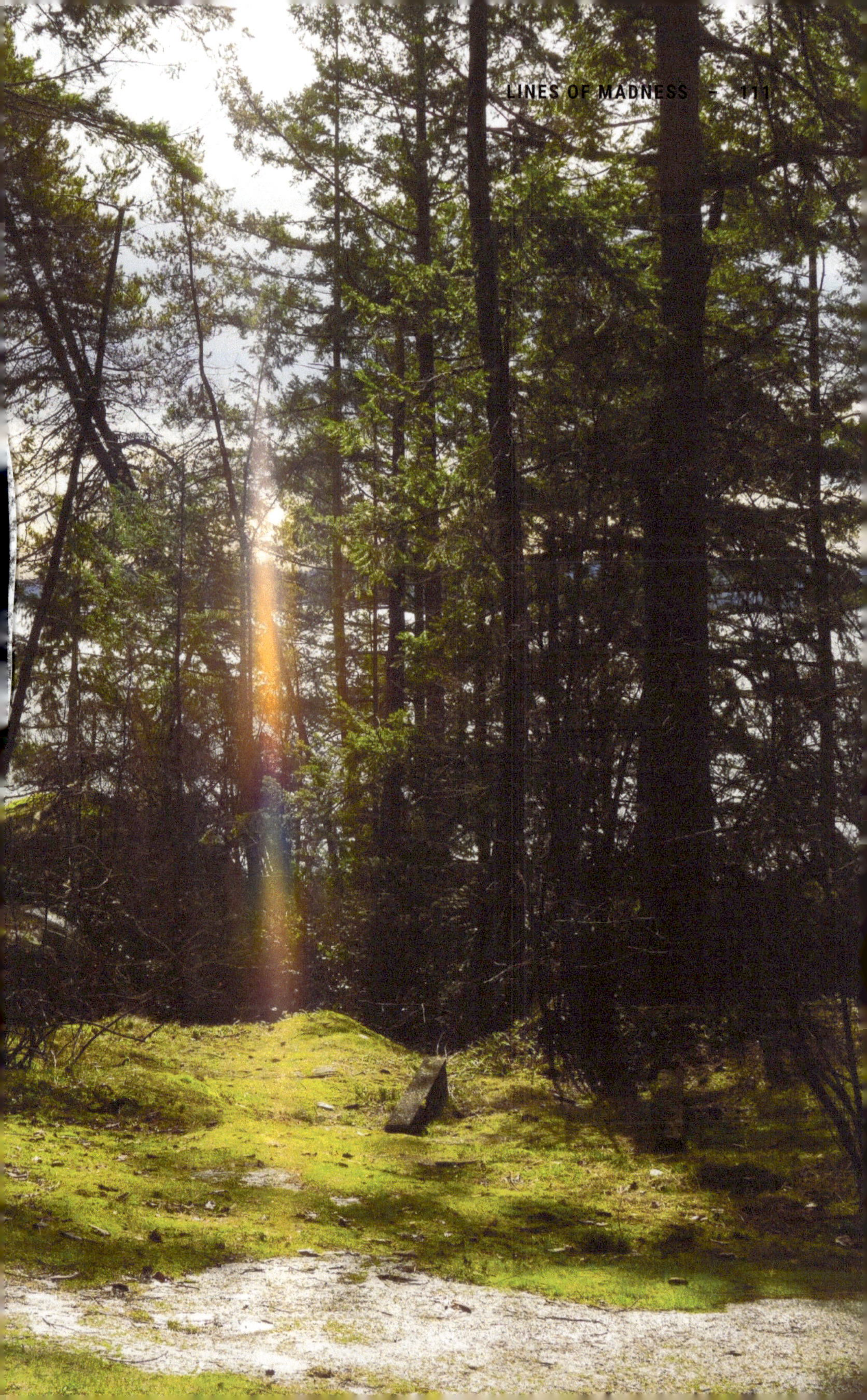

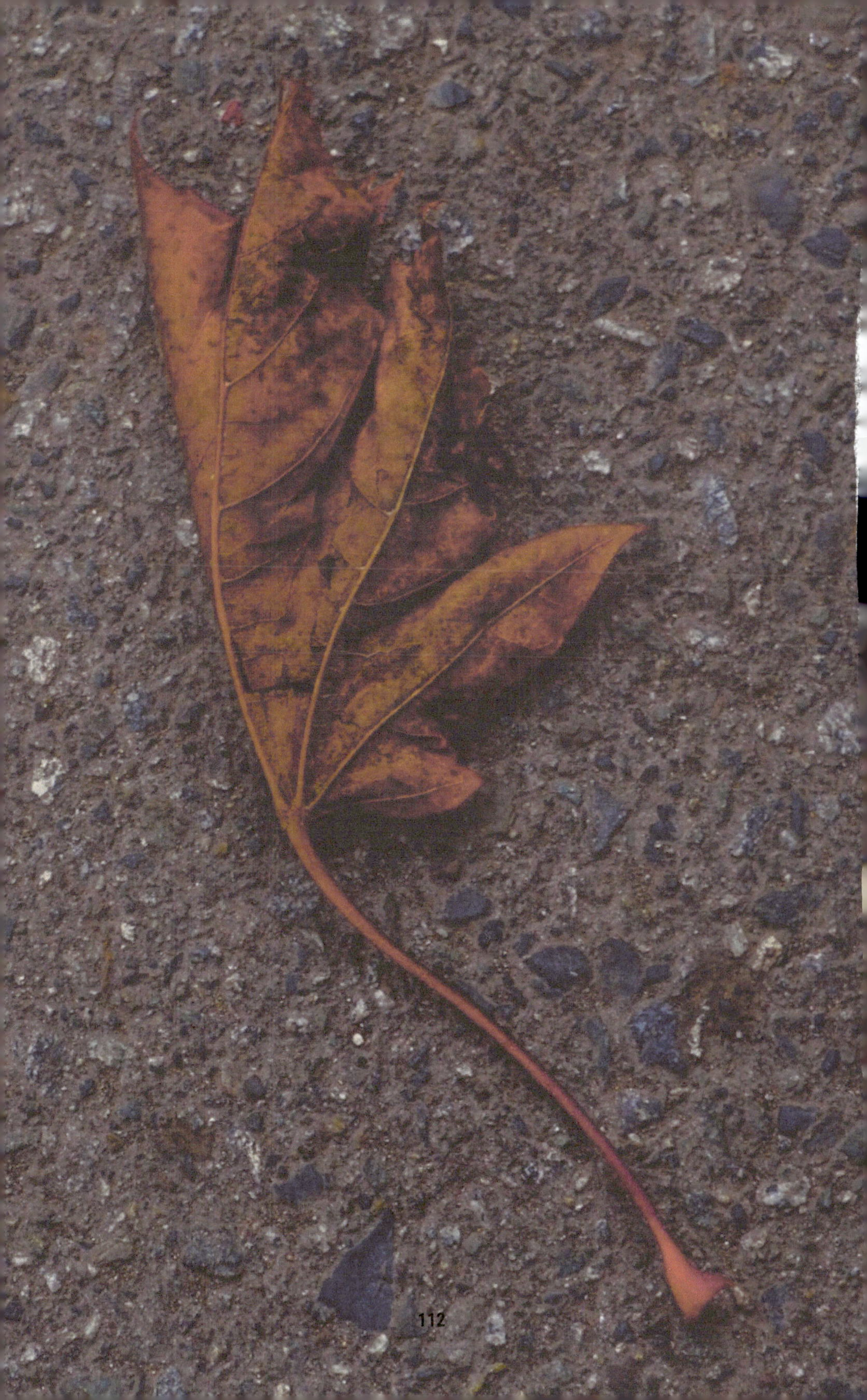

# Darkness

Thoughts of death
fill my mind.

No one sees what
I hide inside.

Hope and joy ripped away
without consent.

I'll never be the same…
Inside and out.

Darkness is how I'm known,
my signature for all eternity.

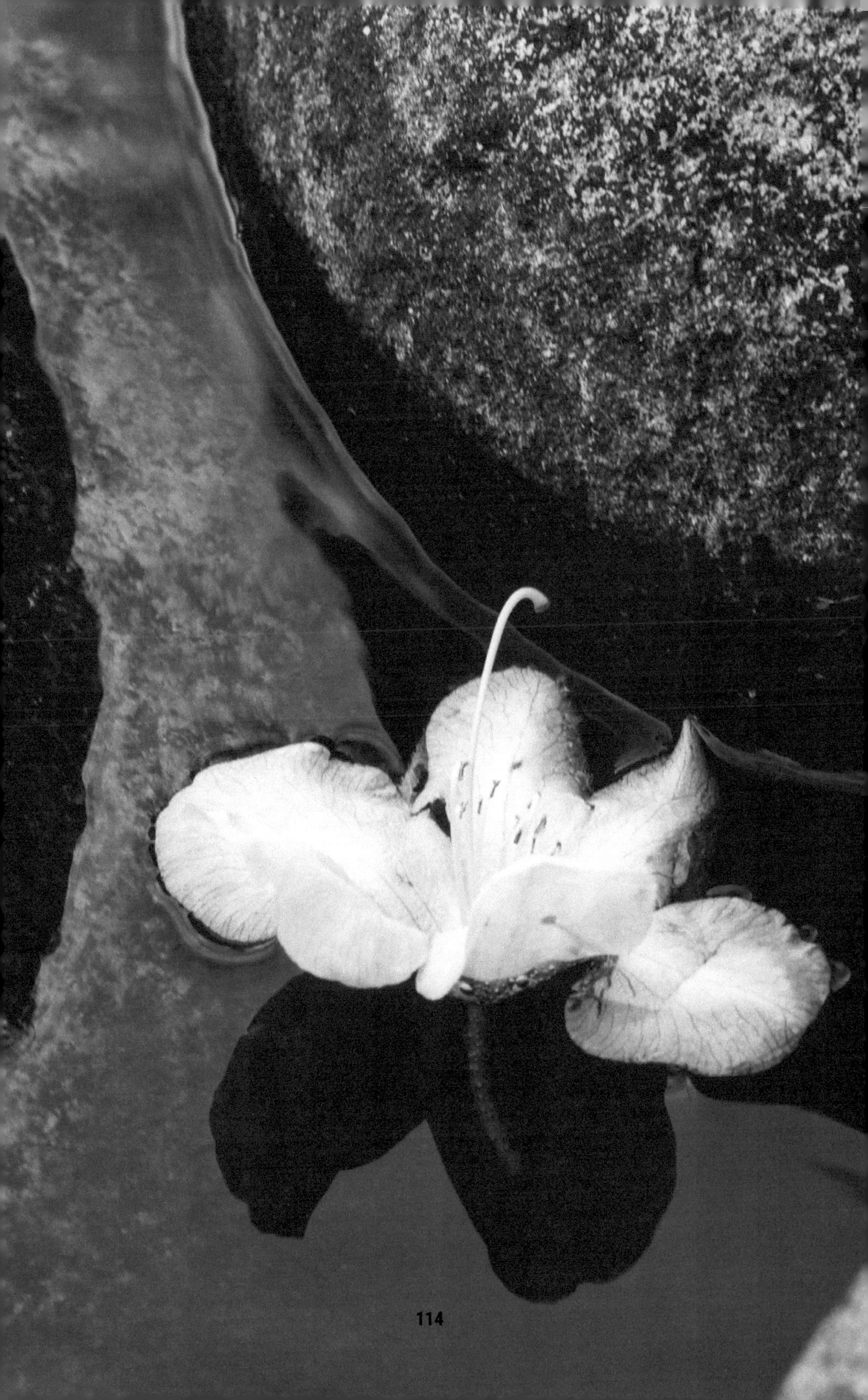

# Piece of Me

Should I write a story,
starting my own identity?
My inner life visible to all.

My joy, my loss, my secrets,
out for others to see.
Will I become a target…
or will hope be shared
as they see my identity?

Each syllable carefully placed,
each sound, a piece of me.
Word by word lines are formed
describing what's inside of me.

These lines are my pain and strength.
Sharing these, I hope
that someone might find
strength to continue fighting
in the midst of adversity.

# Silence

Gentle whimpers turn to sobs.
Shadows looming over me,

defeated…
head spinning...
strangling me.

Heavy sobs chocked away,
empty silence filling me.

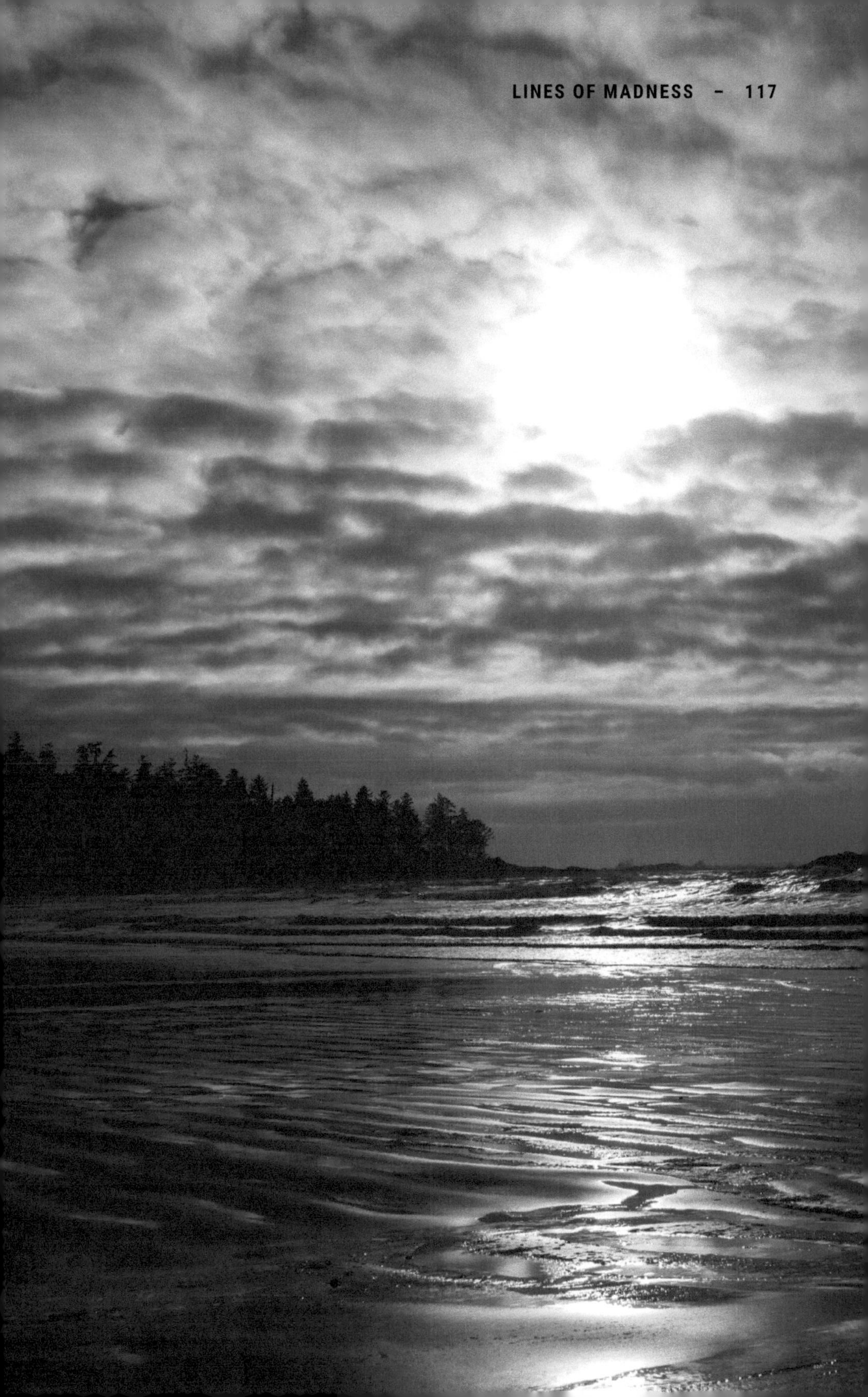

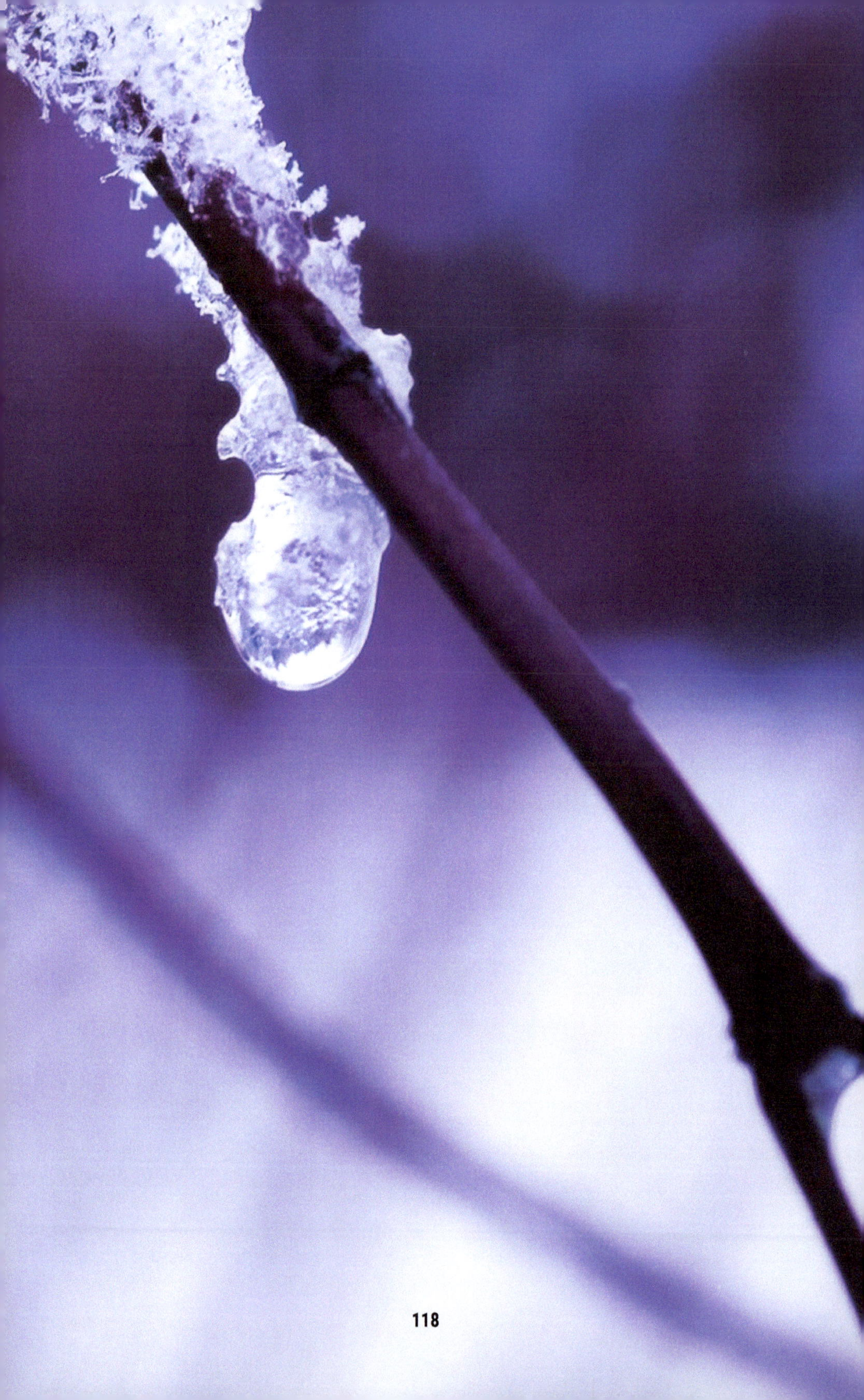

# Time Frozen

Reaching out
I grab my blade.
Time frozen...
it's begun.

Lost,
I cannot look away.
I glide my finger gently
along the edge.
Razor-sharp, to make
the perfect mark.

I hear voices screaming in my head,
"Stop!  Pull back!
You'll regret this!"
Pushing them far away.
No longer can I hear
the cries to save me today.

The blade glides.
Skin so thin.
Blood revealed,
time begins.

# Who am I

I need strength to make it through,
to fight my silent shame away.
I close my eyes, dreaming of being me,
making pride part of my identity.

This path will be long and hard,
but I'm ready inside and out
for the fight to come from myself.
To stand up tall, proud to be me.

# Self Care

I care too much,
holding their pain
like it's my own.

I can't ignore their lives,
their struggles...
they're people, too.

At night I lie awake
thinking of them,
unable to let go
my mind won't stop.

I must separate
their pain from mine.
To take my heart,
and care for me.

Holding my feelings close,
giving time and space
to listen to me.

# The Omen

Fear builds inside my chest.
Mind explodes…
danger approaching.

I can't explain…
no words describe
the dread…
that's filling me.

Lost in time.
Shadows appear
one by one.

One rises,
"I'm here to kill."
Another stands,
"Your family's gone."
Screaming, sobbing,
I try to get away.

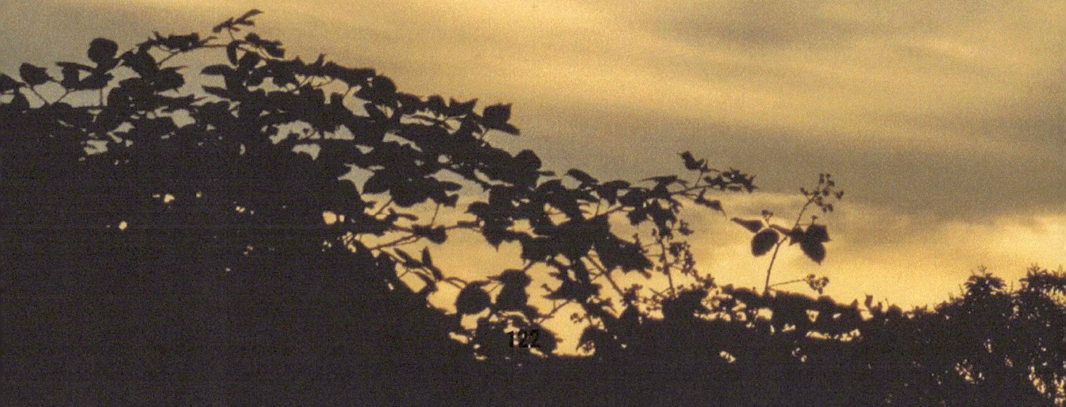

I see a third,
muttering so quietly,
he can barely be heard.

His voice rises,
"Fat — Ugly — Waste,
You — Will — Be — Erased."

The words sear,
my pale skin now charred.
Lightheaded,
knees go weak.

My worst fears come true…
Pain taking over me,
no longer can I fight.

My eyes gaping,
I collapse to the ground,
laying as a shell of
who I once was.

# Bill of Rights

I Have the right to…

1. Listen and be listened to
2. Take breaks when I need
3. Be in control of my body
4. Cry openly, including in public spaces
5. Say no, and be respected
6. Feel my emotions, big and small
7. Choose who I love
8. Be loved
9. Be respected
10. Make my own decisions
11. Love others
12. Follow my own spiritual journey
13. Learn and educate myself
14. Feel mad and angry
15. Express my emotions safely
16. Have enough food to eat and water to drink
17. Have a roof over my head
18. Laugh when I feel like laughing
19. Go to hospital when I need to
20. To take up space in the world
21. Love myself
22. Fart in public
23. Feel safe

24. Miss those I miss, without judgement
25. Spend my money how I want to
26. Communicate my needs
27. Have regular therapy
28. Be sick and take breaks when I need to
29. Reach out for help
30. Be myself
31. Change my mind
32. Be treated with respect
33. Live in a judgement free zone — inside and out
34. Take time for myself
35. Be psychotic and comforted in my fear
36. Choose my occupation
37. Explore my life goals
38. Grieve on my timeline
39. Have a chosen family
40. Feel proud inside
41. Have my Bill of Rights respected

# Emotions

Chaos comes.  Fast I flee.
Fear explodes inside of me.
Cry I do, scream I try,
thoughts begin to fly.

Lost now, deep in thought,
chase them down — I will not.
Thoughts move fast, I anchor more,
racing fast, I slam the door.

Breathe right now, calm will come,
pain explodes, feeling numb.
Hands let go, tensions ease,
ground me now, pain it frees.

Tears still flow, piece by piece,
years of pain will soon cease.
Time goes by, breathe I'm free,
Letting my emotions be.

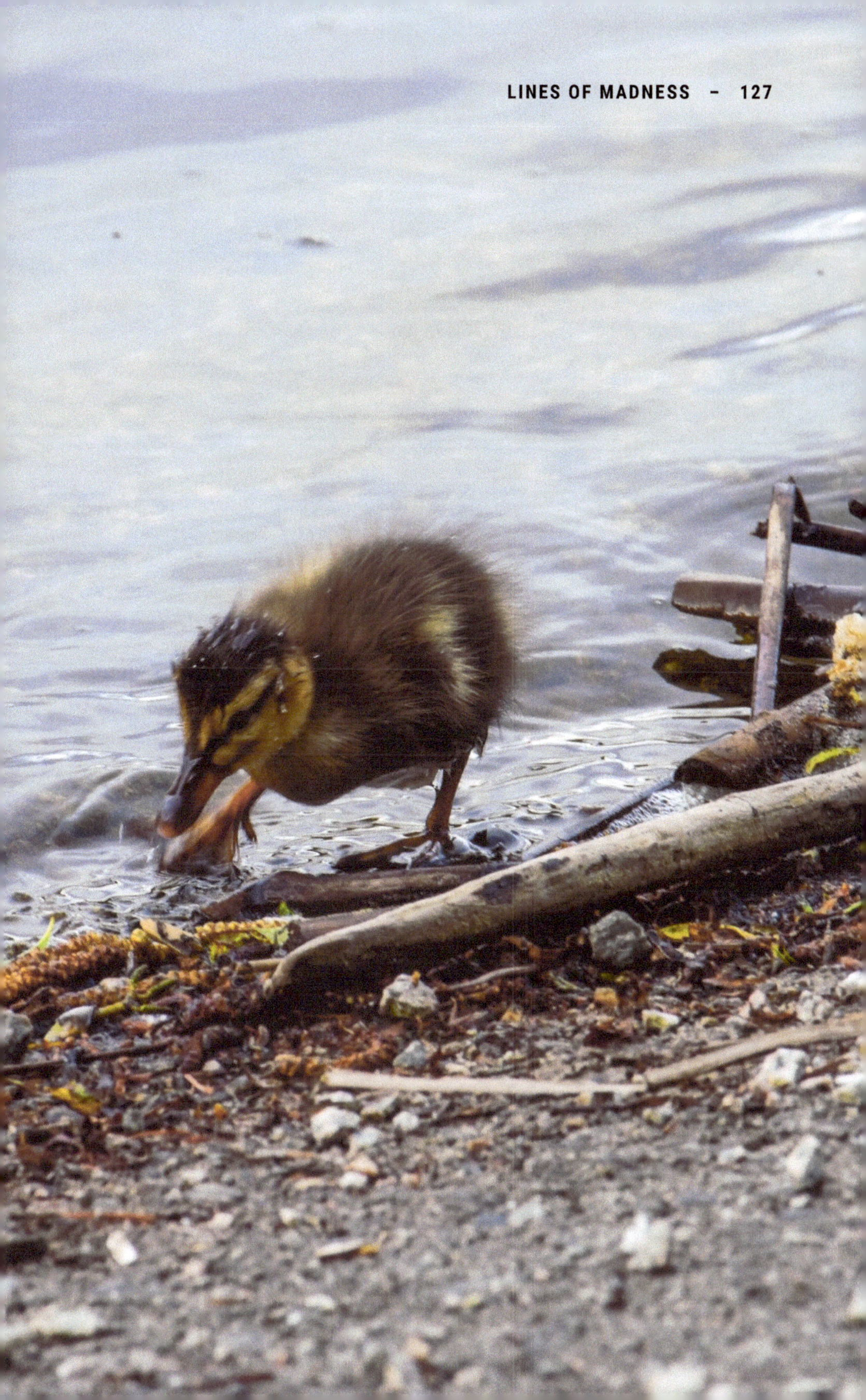

# PRIDE & SHAME

# Failure

Clenching her jaw, she looks at me,
my neck cracks as I drop my head.
She taps her pen on my desk.
I already know that I failed the test.
Toes curling in, as I hold back tears.

"I'm sorr..." –
Her voice stern as she stops me,
"Look me in the eyes"
Each word lasting an eternity,
"I've given up on you,
you have failed me!"

Slamming the test on my desk,
she turns and walks away.
Trembling, I whisper inside,
"I'm Sorry,"
hoping she hears my shame.

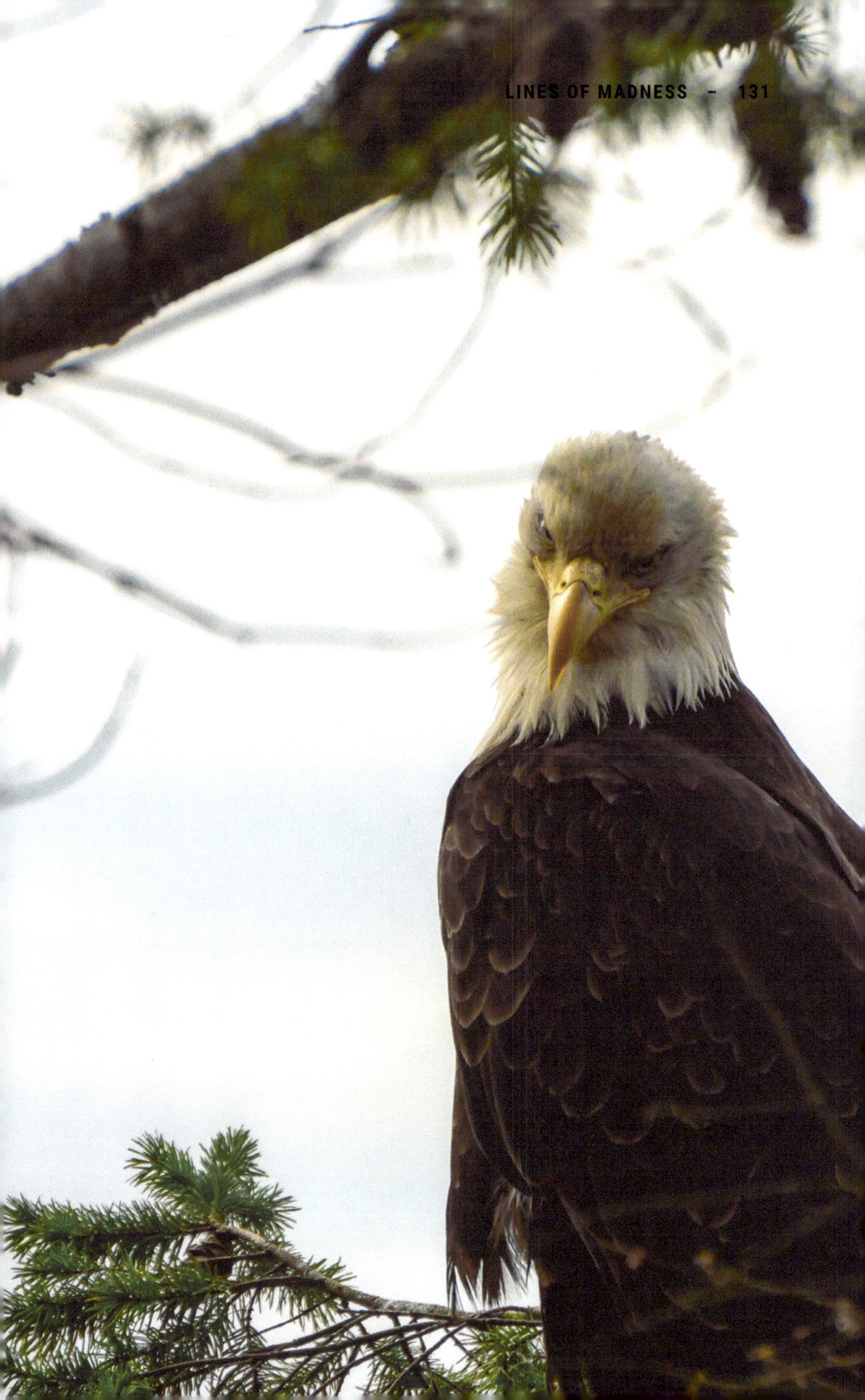

# Big Black Box

I lie in bed,
moaning in pain,
suffocating...
barely able to breathe.

Day breaks,
I sit up,
dizzy…
the room spinning.
I see the big black box
still laying on me.

Pain radiating behind my eyes.
I roll over, struggling to
pull myself out of bed.
This box pulls me to the ground
with a solid thud.

Attached to me,
dragging down everything I do.
I plea, for this box to let me go.
This box is filled with the
weight of my past.

I've barely reached
the bathroom door,
tears of exhaustion flow.

I tell my friends
how I've changed.
They smile gently,
saying that everything is ok,
that nothing is attached to me.

Feeling alone…
I have no hope
of ever being me.

Invisible to others,
lives depression —
a big black box…
chained to me.

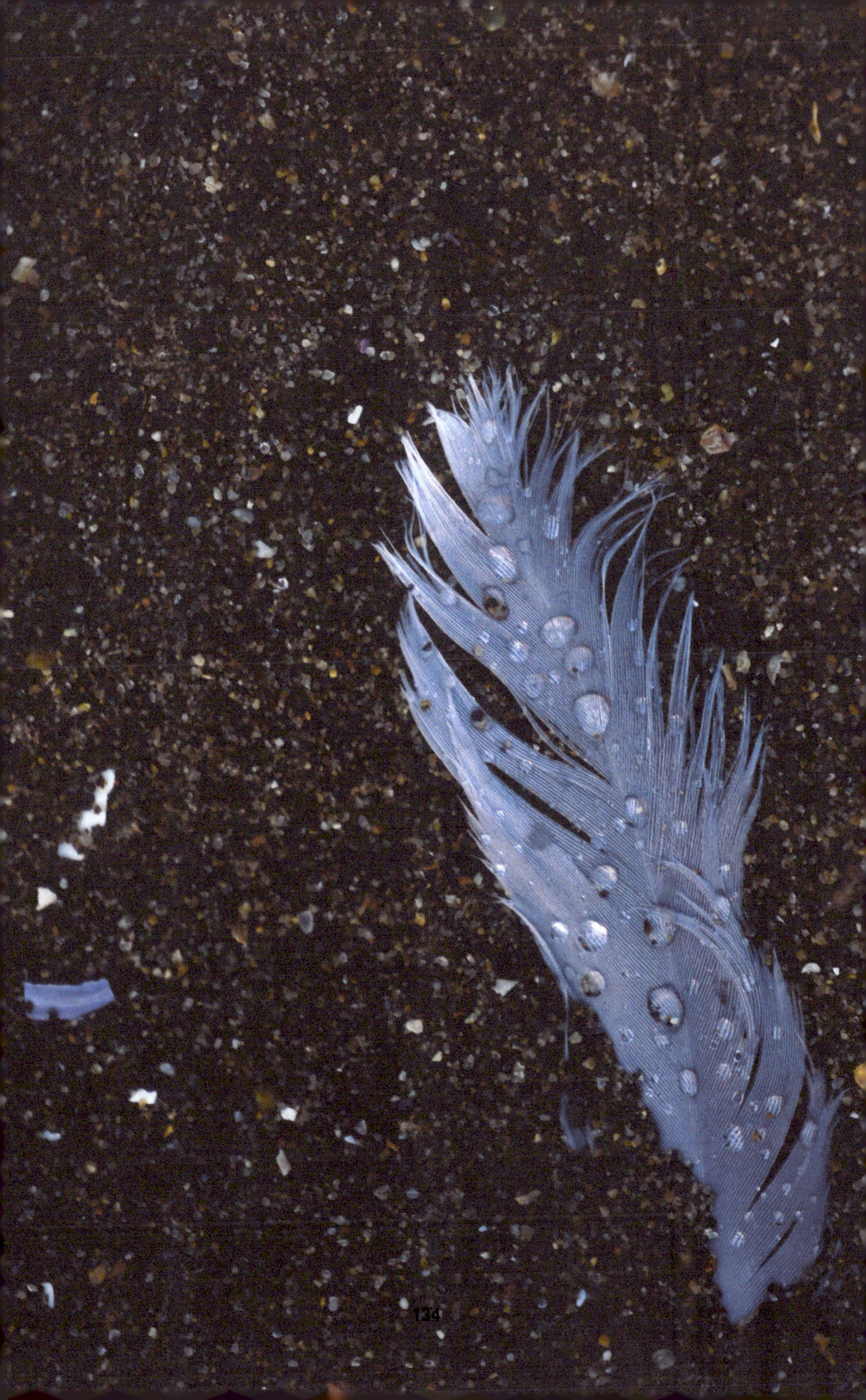

# Blame

Face ashen, terrified to be yourself,
grasping for pride that was ripped away.

Once, a gleam lived in your eyes,
a smile of strength and hope lived strong.

But you are no longer yourself,
you are defiled, filled with impurities.

Blaming yourself, because you are not
proud of the person you have come to be.

# Warrior

Anxiety paralyzed you,
but you fought long and hard...
winning each battle
one by one.

Each day hope grew,
building you up
to be who you are today.

Fighting through fears,
your past has given you strength.
Your dream to be strong has come.
It's time to be yourself,
a warrior, like nothing else.

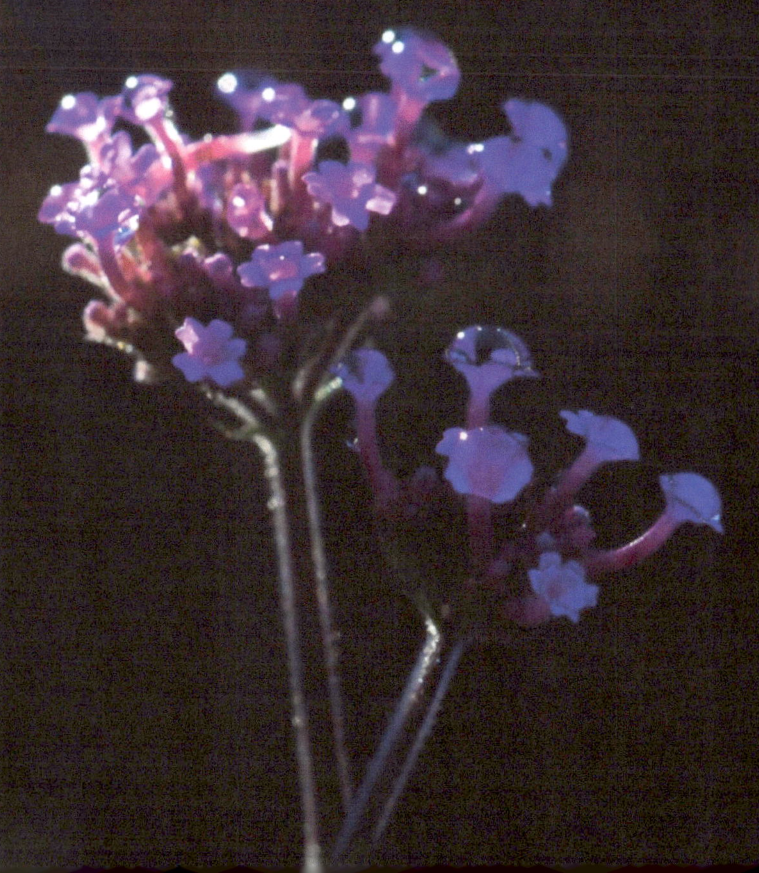

# Stories

There are stories that I make,
making sure they never break.

Covering up,
my pain deep inside.
My arms filled with marks.
Each line skillfully made.

I must devise a story for each,
ensuring they are all unique.

I've drained…
my heart,
my soul,
my hope.

I now tell
the tales of these marks.
Breaking down my deceit.
A life once hidden,
you will know…
my pain,
my tears,
my shame.

Note: Written in diary (Age: 15)

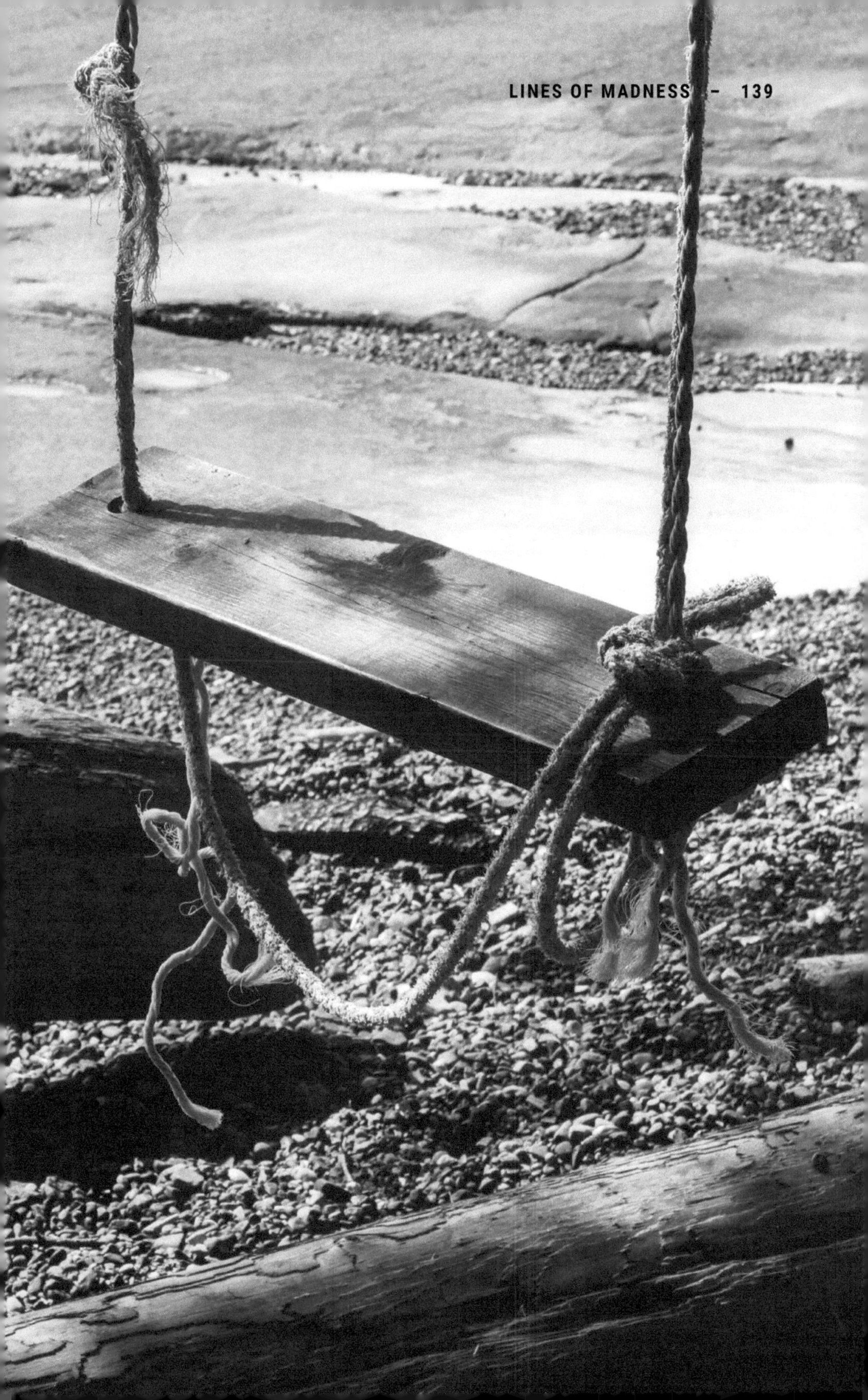

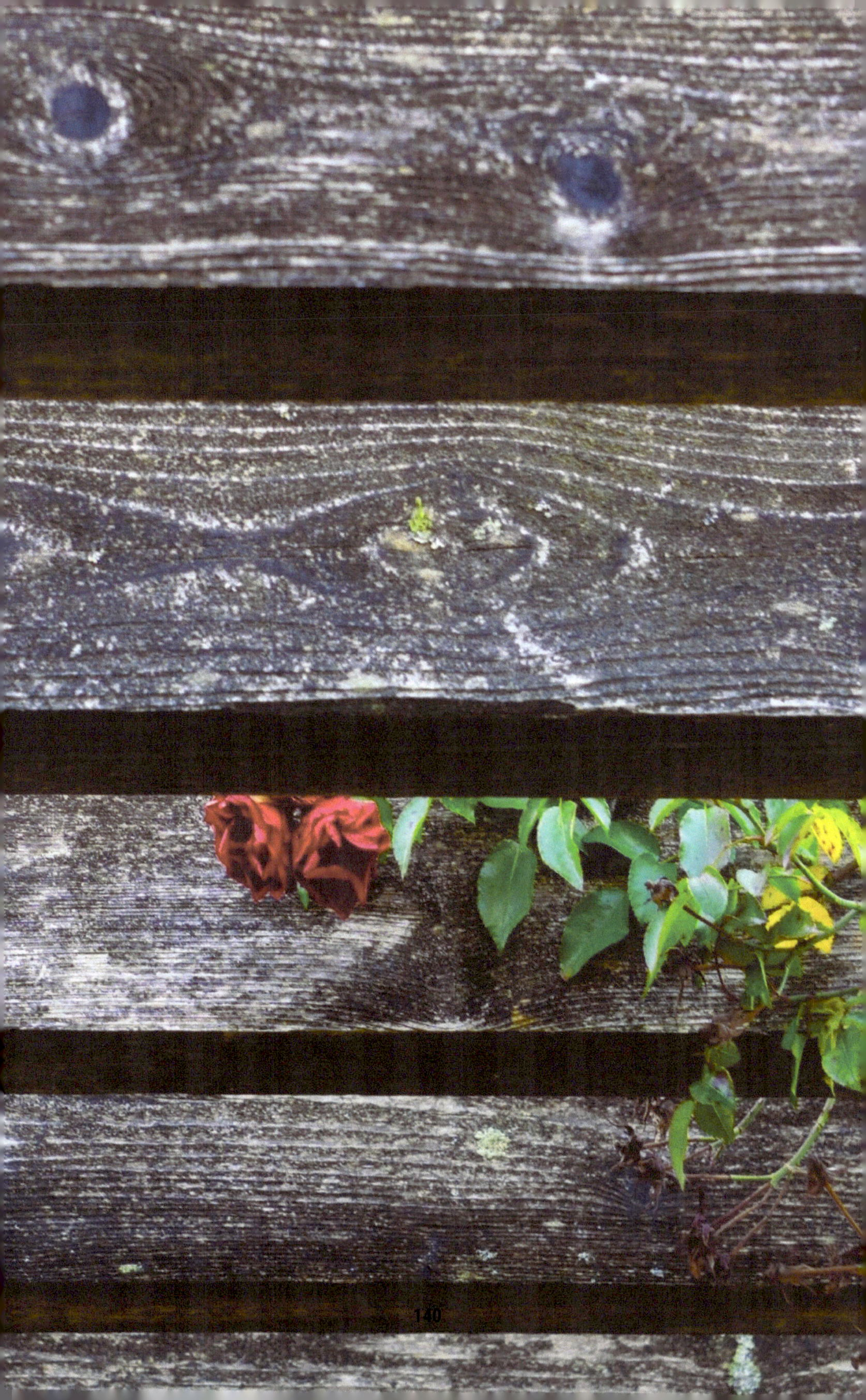

# Demons

Letting out a piercing scream.
Trembling,
I feel them grow.
Trying to engulf me whole.

Faceless beings surrounding me,
coming closer
inch by inch…
Taking over
everything inside of me.

I cannot cry, I cannot look away.
I no longer know who I once was.
The demons have taken away
my identity.

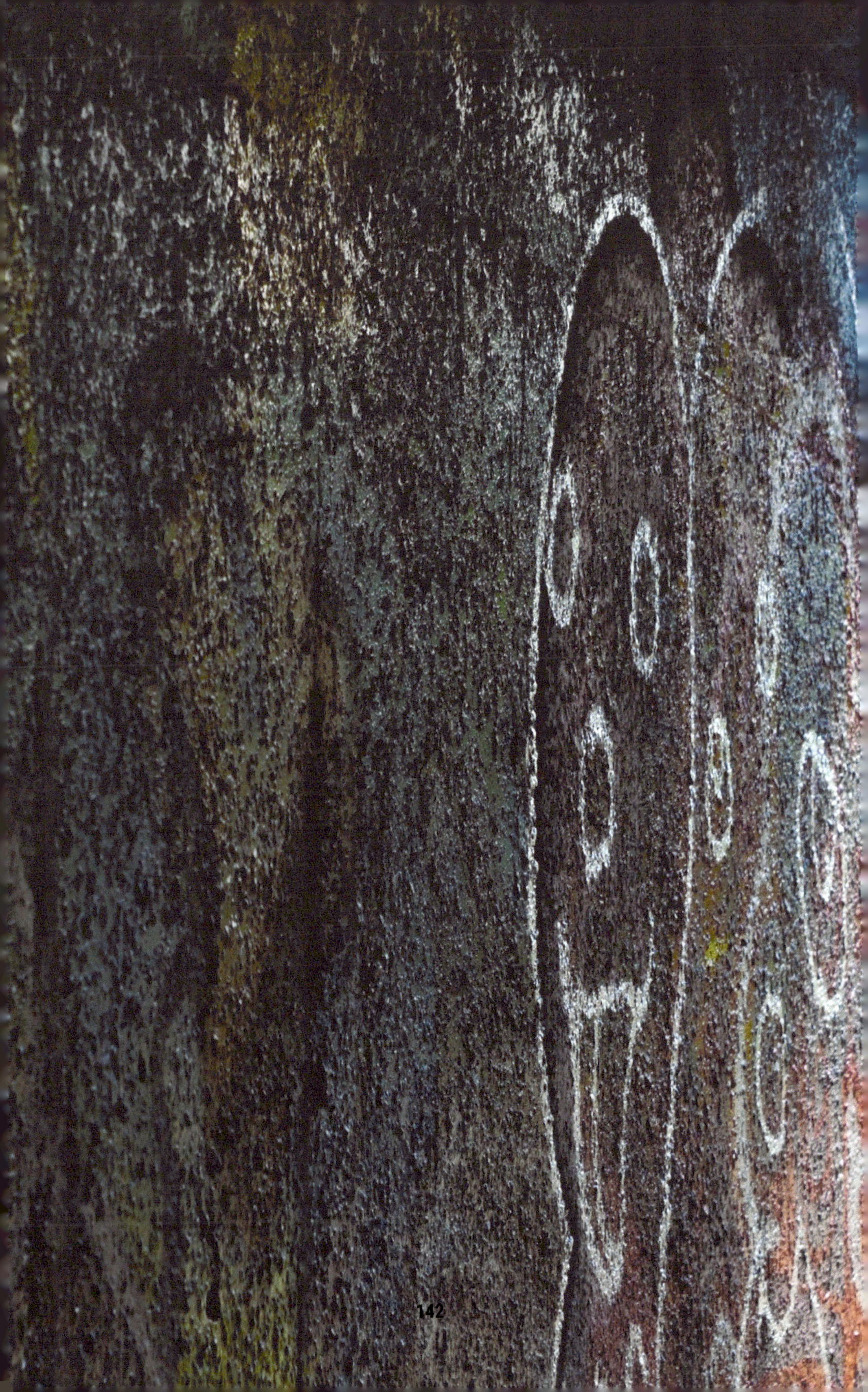

# Toxic Mould

A prisoner, I am.
I've become my pain,
my rights, put on a shelf.

They say I'm a toxic leech,
who will poison the world
if I'm set free.

Darkness, pain and hurt
echo in my mind,
telling me to destroy my skin,
line by line.

A danger to myself,
I can't be free.
There's a horrible person
living inside of me.

Do not approach,
I'm a toxic mould.
Behind locked doors,
I am dirtier
than the hospital floors.

# Black and White

The world is split,
black and white.
It's good,
it's bad.
No grey exists.

I look inside and see
no black,
nor white.
Instead, rainbow plaid
comes to life.

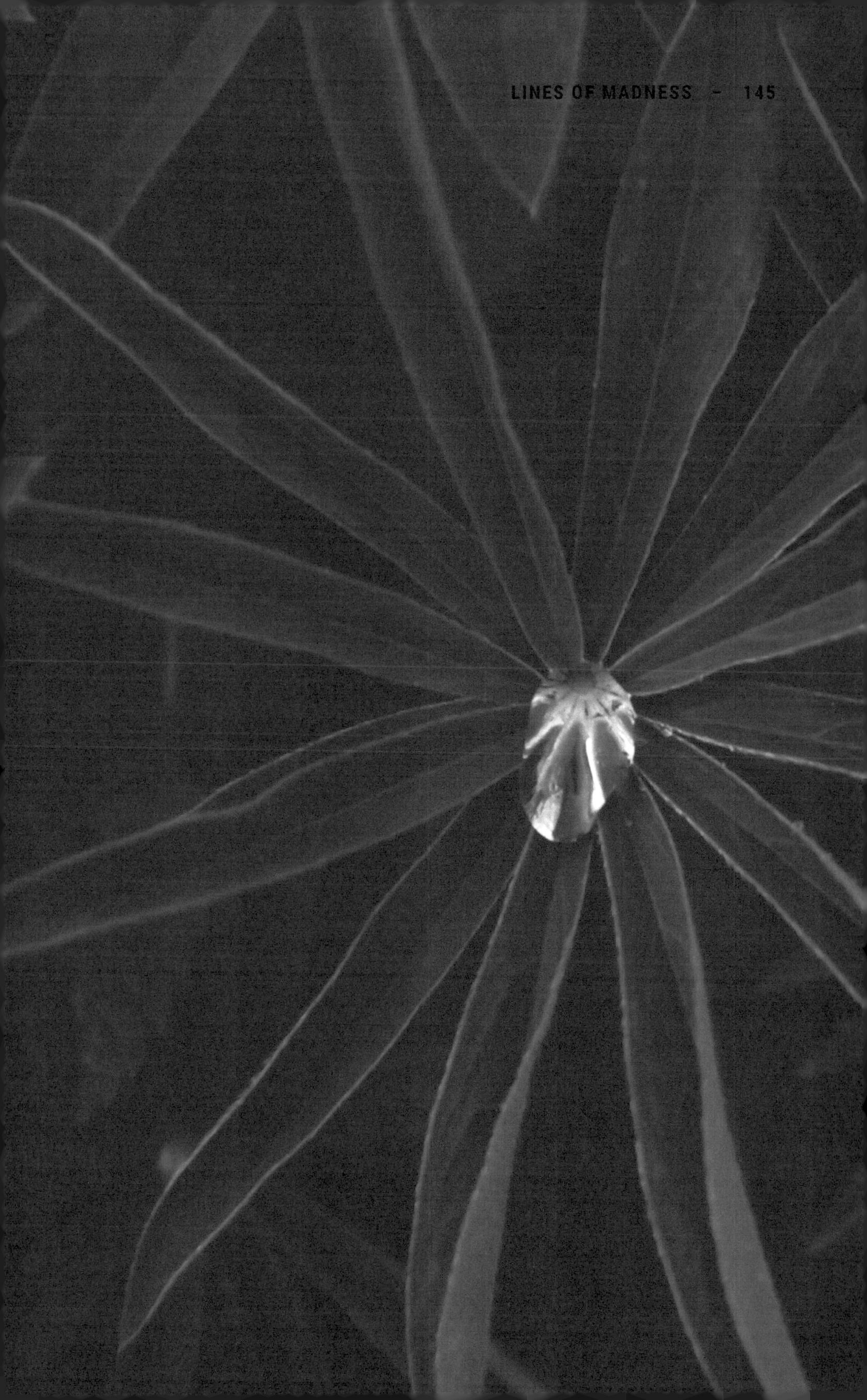

# I Saved a Life

Last night,
I was on the brink death.
Mind screaming,
like a boiling kettle.
Plans of suicide filled my mind.

My heart racing,
chest closing,
body caving,
pain overtaking.

Scrambling, looking for
something, anything,
to help me through the night.

7 years since I last cut,
the pain and shame still etched
stronger than memories.

The pain and blood of the knife
would release the emotions
building inside of me.

Would others understand if
I cut again?

Would they reject me
because of a line on my skin?

Would my family understand
that all I wanted was to live?

The choice:
The bottle of pills to end my life
or a crimson line to live my life.
I made a choice.

Taking the knife,
I carved a mark.
My kettle, now off the stove.

My urge to die easing off.
Last night, cutting saved my life.

# Flying High

Along the sandy beach I run,
my face glowing in the sun!

Sand tickling my big toe,
gripping the string, the faster I go.

Farther and farther, I run,
heading towards the golden sun.

Free at last, my heart soaring,
gleefully laughing and screaming.

My rainbow kite far up in the sky,
I wish I could fly that high.

Proud and free, running in the sand,
my kite soaring above the land.

No one can stop my smile and cheers,
this is the most fun I've had in years.

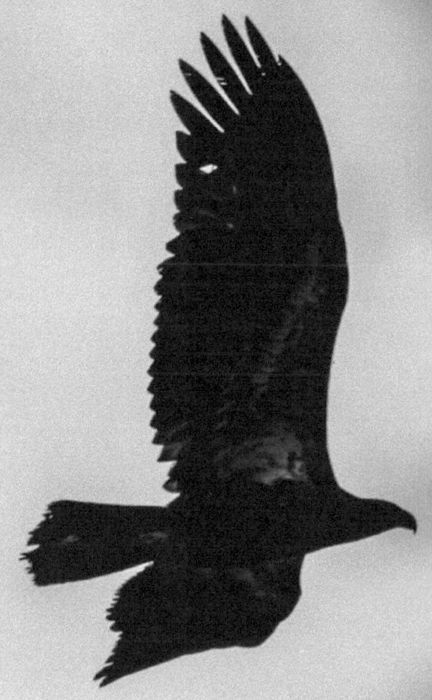

Kaden Pope (they/them) grew up Dawson Creek, BC, located in northern British Columbia with their Mom, Dad and two older siblings. Kaden left home shortly after high school and moved around BC, until calling Vancouver, Canada home. Their mental health journey started early, but due to lack of resources in the North, help was hard to find. They began self harming at age 11 and struggled with depression until things took a turn for the worse. At the age of 23, Kaden began experiencing psychosis and paranoia. Over the next 10 years they were in and out of hospitals, group homes and transitional housing – struggling to find stability. At their worse, Kaden spent over 10 months in hospital out of a 12-month period. They have been certified many times under the Mental Health Act, because they were deemed a danger to themself. They struggled with intense catatonia, psychosis, self harm and suicidal urges. Kaden slowly started improving with the support of family, friends, weekly therapy, medication, ECT (Electroconvulsive Therapy) and an inner drive to want to get better. Kaden now works at a local community college, supporting students with disabilities as they learn how to use Assistive Technology. Kaden still struggles daily with depression and psychosis but has found ways to cope and has built a life worth living. This is Kaden's first book of poetry and photography, and they are excited to share their unique inside look into mental illness with the world.

www.ingramcontent.com/pod-product-compliance
Lightning Source LLC
Chambersburg PA
CBHW040334080726
47599CB00047B/891